Growing Your Own Turtleneck...

and other benefits of aging

Books by Martha Bolton

FROM BETHANY HOUSE PUBLISHERS

Didn't My Skin Used to Fit?

I Think, Therefore I Have a Headache!

Cooking With Hot Flashes

Growing Your Own Turtleneck

It's Always Darkest Before the Fridge Door Opens
(with Phil Callaway)

Your Best Nap Now

Martha Bolton

author of the bestselling *Didn't My Skin Used to Fit?*

Growing Your Own Turtleneck...

and other benefits of aging

Growing Your Own Turtleneck
Copyright © 2005
Martha Bolton

Cover design by Brand Navigation
Cover illustration by Eldon Doty

Published by Bethany House Publishers
11400 Hampshire Avenue South
Bloomington, Minnesota 55438

Bethany House Publishers is a division of
Baker Publishing Group, Grand Rapids, Michigan.

Printed in the United States of America

ISBN   978-0-7642-0003-8

Library of Congress Cataloging-in-Publication Data

Bolton, Martha, 1951-
    Growing your own turtleneck—: and other benefits of aging / by Martha Bolton.
        p.   cm.
    Summary: "Martha Bolton's take on being middle-aged will leave readers laughing out loud and will help you face the day with a smile. This veteran comedy writer adds occasional touching and poignant stories that remind readers what life is all about"—Provided by publisher.
    ISBN 0-7642-0003-8 (pbk.)
    1. Aging—Humor. I. Title.
    PN6231.A43B653   2005
    814'.54—dc22
                                                    2005008947

MARTHA BOLTON is a full-time comedy writer and the author of over fifty books. She was a staff writer for Bob Hope for fifteen years along with writing for Phyllis Diller, Wayne Newton's USO show, Ann Jillian, Mark Lowry, Jeff Allen, and many others. Her material has appeared in *Reader's Digest, Chicken Soup for the Soul* books, and *Brio* magazine, and she has received four Angel Awards and both an Emmy nomination and a Dove Award nomination. Martha and her husband live in Tennessee.

To my loving aunts Sibyl, Clara, and Wilma,
who have stayed forever young, who have never
lost their sense of fun, and who have proved that
true beauty only grows through the years.

Contents

It's Only Right

*It does not require a majority to prevail,
but rather an irate, tireless minority keen to set
brush fires in people's minds.*
—Samuel Adams

It's time. Actually, it's long overdue. They already have them
for parents with young children. They have them for expec-
tant mothers, too. They have them for physically challenged
men and women. While all of this is good and necessary and
certainly helpful, I for one think that it's high time grocery
stores and malls started designating a few parking spaces for
another segment of the population—menopausal women.

Menopausal women could use a little consideration, too,
you know. Do you men and young people have any idea what
driving around a parking lot looking for an available parking
space does to a menopausal woman? Even the streets of Los
Angeles haven't seen that kind of road rage. I once watched a
middle-aged woman hit-and-run three grocery carts, side-
swipe a newspaper stand, and nearly crash into a shelf of pro-
pane tanks just trying to beat an SUV to an open parking

space. Even with all that effort, she still lost the race and stopped right there in the middle of the parking lot and had a good cry. My heart went out to her, but I still didn't move my SUV. In a parking lot situation, it's every menopausal woman for herself!

Before grocery store managers designate these spaces for us, there are a few things they should keep in mind. First of all, a menopausal parking space will need to be extra wide. You know how claustrophobic we hot-flashing women can get in close quarters. We need plenty of room to breathe and move, even if it is outdoors. There's nothing worse than pulling into a parking space and realizing the Volvo next to you has parked so close to the line that you have to climb out of your window and over your hood to exit your car. I would, therefore, suggest the size of these special menopausal spaces be about twice the size of a regular parking space. An RV- or tour-bus-parking size would be just about right. If it can fit a Winnebago, it'll fit a middle-aged hot-flashing woman in a Honda Accord.

Another nice touch that store managers could do would be to circle the spaces with giant fans or misting machines. What menopausal woman wouldn't be moved to tears if she were to open her door and be greeted with gale force winds or a refreshing mist on her way into the store? (I'm getting all weepy just thinking about it.)

But if grocery store managers really want to draw the menopausal crowd to their stores (and let's face it, we baby boomers are quite the shopping force), why not go all out and put our parking spaces *inside* the store, say in the frozen-food aisle. Menopausal women would drive for miles to get to park their car in there and have that blast of frozen-food air hit them the minute they open their car door. Forget double coupons! Forget free tickets to Disneyland! Forget giveaways and contests! Give us arctic air and we'll be loyal customers for life! And really, when you think about it, is getting to park our cars in the frozen-food aisle that much to ask, especially when you consider all the store managers who are already letting children drive those little kiddie carts around in their stores? I guarantee you we'd hit fewer customers with our cars than the kids do with theirs.

Being able to park our cars right in the store would also save us time and energy loading the groceries into the trunk or the back of our SUVs. All we would have to do is drive our car up to the check-out counter, pay the bill, put the bagged groceries directly into our car, and then drive away.

But designated parking spaces at grocery stores is only the beginning. I would also like to suggest that officials at the Department of Transportation begin looking into the possibility of adding a special "menopause lane" to all our interstate highways. I realize this could get pricey and on the surface might appear to involve some tax hikes to pay for it, but hear me out. It's a known fact that menopausal women sometimes have difficulty making decisions, am I right? Wait, maybe I shouldn't say that. Aw, why not? It's my book. No, wait. It's a generalization and . . . Oh, never mind, I'm going to leave it in because it's true. We do have trouble making decisions. A separate menopause lane would help us with this indecisiveness because there would be an off-ramp every five hundred feet or so to accommodate last-minute exit decisions of the menopausal woman. The resulting decrease in car accidents due to multiple and unsafe lane change attempts should defray the cost of adding such a lane. And think of the gasoline savings. Here in the South if you miss your off-ramp, you sometimes have to drive an extra ten or fifteen miles before you can get off the highway and reverse your direction. That's a lot of unnecessary fuel we menopausal drivers are wasting just because we can't make up our minds in time to exit when we're supposed to. So in actuality, a menopause lane would be saving the country both money and precious fuel. If we as a nation are truly seeking to lessen our dependence on foreign oil, adding several extra off-ramps would be one way to help us achieve this goal. So a tax hike wouldn't even be needed because the menopause lane would pay for itself over time.

And there are even more benefits to a menopause lane. You know how we menopausal women tend to be forgetful? How many times has one of us driven in the fast lane from, say, San Diego to San Francisco with our left-turn signal blinking the entire way? Well, if we were restricted to driving in our own menopause lane, that sort of behavior wouldn't bother any of the other drivers. No one would think twice about our turn signal staying on for one hundred, two hundred, even five hundred miles. They would simply see what lane we were driving in, nod their heads sympathetically, and say under their breath, "Ah, the menopause lane. Of course." The same thing goes if we happen to be zooming along with a can of soda or our purse sitting on the roof of our car.

Other drivers might notice it, but instead of pointing and laughing, like they do now, they would once again notice what lane we are driving in and cut us some slack.

The signage for these lanes would be important. Aside from the Menopause Lane signs, I propose that the only other signs allowed in our special lane would be: Wind Gusts Next Five Miles. What hot-flash suffering fifty-year-old woman wouldn't love five miles of wind gusts? All Turn Off Air-Conditioning Next Five Miles signs, however, like the ones they post before steep inclines, would be strictly prohibited. Forcing a menopausal woman to turn off the air-conditioning in her car for any distance should be considered life endangerment and tossed out of the vehicular code in all states anyway.

The menopause lane should also be exempt from speed limit signs. Speed limit signs only confuse us. How many menopausal women have been pulled over by a patrol officer simply because they had inadvertently gotten the highway number and the speed limit signs mixed up? For you young people or men reading this, I can assure you that this is easier to do than you might realize. You see, when a menopausal woman glances at a highway number sign, all she sees is the number and can easily assume that it's referring to the speed limit. When you're in the middle of a hot flash, you're not always thinking clearly. I've inadvertently mixed up highway number signs and speed limit signs myself on many occasions. It doesn't matter much if you're on Interstate 40, but you should see how quickly people get out of your way on the 210!

But why stop with parking spaces and extra lanes? Banks would also do well to offer their customers a separate menopause banking line. Let them keep one roped-off line for their regular customers, but over by the air-conditioning ducts they could rope off another line for all of us menopausal customers. This line would have its own special teller, too—one who has been specially trained in menopause management. Let's face it, menopause customers need special consideration when it comes to banking. We sometimes forget whether check #485 was written for our house payment of $1294.00 or to the paper boy for $12.94. It's a minor mix-up, but believe me, it can really mess up your accounting. By helping us with problems like this, bank managers would also be helping the community. How many times does a non-menopausal customer get stuck in line behind an estrogen-deprived woman who is sobbing uncontrollably and holding up the line because her checks arrived in the mail with the wrong cartoon character printed on them? Other customers don't understand these emotional outbursts. To them the woman's outburst seems irrational, so they get impatient with her. But menopausal customers understand. In a menopause line she would receive the empathy and patience she needs. In fact, everyone in the menopause line would probably be crying along with her.

Banks should offer us our own menopause credit cards, too. These would look a lot like a regular credit card, except they would come with a warning to salesclerks: *Menopausal customer. Confront about over-credit-line limits at your own risk.*

And for gold accounts, the card would come with its own mini-fan attached to it.

Churches could do their part, too, by offering a custom menopause hymnal for their middle-aged parishioners. Many of the hymnals that are on the market right now were compiled by men. Men don't always understand the needs of the menopausal church woman. Menopausal women might not feel all that comfortable singing songs like "All Consuming Fire" and "Roll On, O Billow of Fire." While these are classic and inspiring hymns, we're already hot enough. We'd much rather be singing songs like "There Shall Be Showers of Blessing," "Send Down the Rain," "Cool Water," and "This, Too, Shall Pass."

And don't even get me started on department store dressing rooms. Menopausal women have wanted and deserved their own mirrorless, low-lit dressing rooms for years. But have department store managers listened to us? No. In fact, most of them have done the exact opposite. With each new swimsuit season it seems they add even more mirrors and brighter lights to these cubicles of terror. I went in one the other day that was so brightly lit it made me feel like I was changing clothes in the middle of a nighttime highway construction site. Come to think of it, I probably could have used some of the heavy equipment to help me get that swimsuit on!

The bottom line is this: Today's menopausal woman should be receiving far more attention and consideration than she is currently getting. We're human beings, too, with needs and feelings. Yes, we have hot flashes that make us spontaneously combust on a regular basis, and our night sweats can turn us into a water show, sprouting fountains of liquid in all directions in a matter of minutes, nearly drowning our house pets and any small children who happen to walk by. But none of that is our fault. It's not our fault if we have the natural ability to turn into a heat lamp at any given moment, capable of warming a 20' × 20' patio in four minutes flat. It's not our fault if we cry because Grape-Nuts just went on sale. It's not our fault if we care about the cartoon character that's on our checks. There are strange things happening inside our bodies that we have absolutely no control over.

So instead of judging us for all of these changes, why not offer us some support? Why not become politically active on our behalf? Why not join with us in our cause and help us at long last get our due? Write a letter to the Department of Transportation and suggest that a menopause lane be added to all the highways of this nation. Speak with your local banker about adding a separate line for their menopausal customers. Take our mission out of the shadows and force the world to quit ignoring our needs. Help us to organize our Million Menopausal Women March all the way to the White House and to the front steps of Congress. I realize that Washington, D.C., can get humid, and the thought of all of us crowded together marching as one through the streets in that hot, muggy air is what is keeping most of us from committing, but it's time to grab a sweatband and just go. It's time we menopausal women became a force to be reckoned with. It's time we formed our own club, like the red hat ladies, only sweatier.

And maybe it's finally time to elect a hot-flashing, night-sweating menopausal woman as president! What enemy in their right mind would take on an estrogen-deprived woman that close to the red phone? Talk about a homeland security plan!

The possibilities are endless. All it will take is for us to organize. But then again, on second thought, let's just stay at home in front of a fan.

> **I am extraordinarily patient, provided I get my own way in the end.**
> —Margaret Thatcher

Midnight at the Oasis

What I dream of is an art of balance, of purity and serenity devoid of troubling or depressing subject matter—a soothing, calming influence on the mind, rather like a good armchair which provides relaxation from physical fatigue.
—Henri Matisse

The first chapter dealt with middle-aged women. Now it's the man's turn.

Men, are you aware that there is a recliner chair on the market right now called the Oasis? This super plush, over-stuffed chair is being hailed as the ultimate recliner. With a span of forty-one inches from arm to arm, there is also a built-in remote control, a cup holder for one soda, and a thermoelectric cooler that holds up to six more cans! And that's not all. There is also an in-chair telephone, a six-point massager and heat system (for when you don't want to get up to turn down the air-conditioning), and for all of you sports fans, the chair is even available in your favorite team colors.

As good as this chair is, I still I think I could have designed an even better recliner. My idea of the perfect recliner would be one that has its own trash compactor large enough to handle pizza boxes and giant bags of stale popcorn. It would also have a super-powered garden hose complete with water hookup so you could just open the door and water your yard without ever leaving your seat. Or maybe I should go one better and make the chair a combination recliner/riding lawn mower. At half time, guys could press a button and ride out into the yard and mow some of the lawn before the game starts up again.

My chair would also have an indoor rotisserie/grill so men could cook dinner from the comforts of their chair. And since there would already be the water hookup for the garden hose, I could even add a shower head attachment to go along with it, and maybe a mirror so men could shower and shave and not miss a single play in the game. A computer with broadband connection would be a nice addition, too, as well as a FedEx drop box, in case he needed to mail anything. And like the overhead compartment on an airplane, the chair would have a compartment for storing extra pillows and blankets, too. And there would be a miniature refrigerator big enough to hold six-foot-long submarine sandwiches.

Another plus for many husbands would be for the chair to have rear- and side-view mirrors so they can see when their wife is entering the room with her honey-do list. This way, the men can pretend to be napping.

And finally, the chair would have a lightning rod, just in

case a severe thunderstorm ever rolls through; it would not so much deflect the electricity from a bolt of lightning as channel the natural energy to jump-start the tanning bed attachment.

Now *that* is a chair!

Sound too good to be true? Who knows, maybe someday La-Z-Boy or some other manufacturer will come out with a recliner like that. If they do, I have a feeling it'll be on every man's Christmas wish list. That is, until the recliner/fishing boat comes along. Or the recliner/twin-engine airplane. Or the . . . well, it's obvious the possibilities are endless.

Laziness is nothing more than the habit of resting before you get tired.
—Jules Renard

The Five People You Meet in a Buffet Line

Give me liberty or . . . OOOooo . . . A jelly donut!
—Homer Simpson

There is a book that has been receiving all sorts of critical acclaim. It's called *The Five People You Meet in Heaven,* and it has spent months on *The New York Times* Best-Seller list. They even made a television movie out of it. Now, while I'm sure it is a wonderful book, I can't help but wonder about all the notable people who aren't in the book—the people we don't hear much about. Like, what about the five people you meet, say, in a buffet line? Has anyone ever written a book about them? No. So once again the task has fallen to me. I may not be able to fill an entire book about these five noble souls, but the least I can do is dedicate a chapter to them.

Before I begin describing them to you, though, I must

confess that I myself am a buffet person. I happen to love buffets. I fully understand the urge to eat that third plate of food even after you've already unbuttoned, unbuckled, and halfway unzipped everything that can possibly be unbuttoned, unbuckled, and unzipped on your person. I understand the quest to get every penny of your seven dollars and ninety-nine cents' worth. Not everyone understands this compulsion, but I do. And I can certainly identify with the overwhelming need to scoop fourteen different casseroles onto your plate and enough dinner rolls for a party of eight. It's an unseen force that drives us to do these sorts of things. It is not an option, and I understand this.

Like all buffet people, I, too, have pondered the mysteries of the pudding trays, wondering how those stray peas found their way in there. I have survived tong fights with other customers over the last chicken drumstick. And I have on numerous occasions eaten crab salad that is spelled with a *k*, never once asking the question, "So what kind of fish is this *really*?"

Yes, I am a buffet person down to my very core, and I am proud of it. I am a dedicated and experienced partaker of the mac and cheese. I have been one with the corn fritter. I have piled my food so high as to interfere with the operation of the ceiling fans. I have scooped and dipped and grabbed and reached with the best of them. And on those rare occasions when I've had to stop at only my second plate of food (or roughly 40,000 calories), I have even endured ridicule by other, even more dedicated buffet people who have mercilously jeered me with cutting, hurtful labels like "buffet wimp" and "plate-o-phobe."

I say all of this so that you will know my point of reference. This is not a case of an outsider looking in. These are the words of someone who has held on to her fork until the waitstaff has had to unwrap her clutched fingers from around it. I am a buffet connoisseur, an all-you-can-eat maven, a dedicated defender of the potato and taco bar. In other words, I know whereof I speak.

Now for those of you who have never been to Branson, Missouri; Pigeon Forge, Tennessee; or basically anywhere in the South, and have yet to experience the world of the buffet, a brief definition of the buffet would be in order before we proceed any further. For one thing, buffets are different from cafeterias. At a cafeteria, you pay for each individual item on your tray. That can get expensive. You take a dish of corn, a scoop of mashed potatoes and gravy, a couple of chicken wings, and a slice of apple pie, and before you know it, your meal has cost you $27.98. You could have eaten steak and lobster for that amount of money, and not had to carry your own tray to the table.

For this reason, I feel that the buffet is better than a cafeteria. The rules of the buffet are quite simply that you are free to eat whatever you can possibly consume for one low price. It's all yours for the taking. Eat as much or as little as you want and there will never be any surprises when you get the bill. You know exactly what you're going to pay before you scoop out your first helping of fried okra.

Buffets are also different from meat-and-threes. Meat-and-threes are big here in the South, too. A meat-and-three is just that—one meat item and three vegetable choices for one low price. Some meat-and-threes offer a smaller version, the meat-and-two, for those of us on a diet. (For the diet plate, they only ladle one cup of gravy over your mashed potatoes instead of two.)

For my money, I feel the buffet is the best value. Why settle for only three sides when a buffet gives you your choice of twenty-six? Sometimes it's even more. And believe me, seeing all the different and creative ways they can use a pasta noodle is worth the price of admission.

Buffets are getting so popular right now that some unusual places are beginning to offer them—places like gas stations. I know that sounds odd, but it's true. Just drive along any interstate in the South, and you're sure to see a gas station advertising an all-you-can-eat buffet. Now, I'm not endorsing these buffets, nor am I warning you against them. I'm simply letting you know they are there. But I do have to say that getting gas where you get gas does sound a bit unnatural to me.

Wherever you find a buffet, though, one thing is certain— you're sure to meet the following five people.

First, there's *Muu Muu Mama*. Anyone who has ever been to a buffet has seen Muu Muu Mama. She is serious about her buffet experience. The muu muu she's wearing may or may not match her house slippers, but whatever you do, don't get in Muu Muu Mama's way. She is one determined soul and has elbowed her way past the best of them. You are a mere mortal and no match for such speed and agility. Just as you reach for the corn-bread dressing, quick as a flash she beats you to it. Reach for some steamed carrots, and she's already got her hand on the spoon. Go for the turnip greens, and she appears out of nowhere and scoops some onto her plate first. She has the reflexes of a Wild West gunfighter and the cunning of a stealth fighter pilot. She'll beat you every time. And she's the master of disguise. She may look like a size eighteen under all of that flowing material, but Muu Muu Mama weighs in at less than a hundred pounds. She just wears the muu muu so that when she leaves, she can sneak out thirty pounds of muffins for later.

Next, there's *Finger-Licking Freddie*. Watching Finger-Licking Freddie is like watching a ballet. As he dishes out his food, it's *The Nutcracker Meets Emeril* or *Swan Lake Meets Uncle Ben*. First he scoops some potatoes and gravy onto his plate, then gracefully raises his arm upward to lick his fingers. Without missing a beat, he steps lightly down the aisle and dishes up some salad. Some of the ranch dressing happens to drip down the side of his plate, but not to worry. Finger-Licking Freddie simply slides his finger along the rim, then gracefully licks his fingers again. He makes a quarter turn and moves on to the meat station. Some au jus drips onto his palm. He licks it up, does a turn to grab a roll, and sneaks a lick of the freshly melted butter on top of it. He scoops and licks so much that by the time he makes it to the last food station, he's already consumed eighteen hundred calories! But anyone who has been watching him is ready to applaud. Every move has been the epitome of grace and style and perfectly timed to the music playing over the intercom.

It's every bit as entertaining as any ballet you'll ever see. And I'm pretty sure the overalls are a lot easier on the circulation than ballet tights.

Chicken Wing Darla is the lady who will eat an entire tray of chicken wings, sucking every molecule of meat out of each one, stacking the ravaged bones onto her plate like a pile of greasy firewood. When you consider she's only working with four teeth, it's quite a feat. Frankly, I try to leave a little bit of meat on my chicken bones just out of respect. I figure if the animal laid down his life for my lunch, the least I can do is leave him a little dignity . . . and gristle.

Buffet Charley has hit every buffet east of the Mississippi, and you can tell. Like the state stickers that my parents used to stick to the windows of our station wagon to show people everywhere we'd been, Buffet Charley has the same idea, only he does it with gravy stains.

"See that one there? That's the sausage gravy I had down in Florida. And that one over there? That's the turkey and giblet gravy I had in Kansas. And that one right there, well, that's the country white gravy and mashed potatoes I had out west in Texas." He samples gravy like a wine expert tastes wine, taking a mouthful and swishing it around in his mouth. *"Ah, good texture. Full bodied and rich. No lumps. I would say it was made on Tuesday. Ah, yes, Tuesday, a very good day."*

Juggling Jimmy is the last of the five. Juggling Jimmy is easy to spot because of all the plates he juggles as he makes his way around the food stations. When you first see him, you're impressed because you think he's getting food for his wife and kids. *How sweet,* you think to yourself, *and so consid-*

erate. You might even chastise your own husband with a kick under the table or a dinner roll to the head, *"Why don't you ever do that for me, Harry?!"*

But as your eyes follow Juggling Jimmy, now with four plates and several dessert cups, all the way back to his seat, you notice that this guy is eating alone. Every single one of those plates are for him. Now you have to eat those words you said to your husband, but you're already so full you don't think you can squeeze in another bite, much less nine words and punctuation. But you do it because you have no choice. The truth is inescapable. Juggling Jimmy, like all the others, just enjoys getting his money's worth. He enjoys it so much, in fact, that he often times his arrival to be toward the end of the lunch buffet and just before they switch over to the dinner menu. He'll eat lunch, then sit around visiting with the other customers until the dinner buffet is put out. Then he'll get up and start with four plates all over again. He figures he's beating the system by getting two meals for the price of one, and no one is the wiser. People like Juggling Jimmy and Muu Muu Mama make you wonder how buffets can make any profit at all. But then, I suppose there are plenty of finicky adolescents who only take gelatin and crackers and their parents still have to pay $7.99 for them. So maybe it all evens out.

And there you have it—The Five People You Meet in a Buffet Line. There are other buffet people, of course. CEOs and plumbers, doctors and gardeners, business owners and retirees—all good people, every one. People who like to get a good value for their money, and maybe some extra muffins on the side. Muu Muu Mama and Juggling Jimmy are technically breaking the buffet rules, of course, but most of the time the FBI is too busy to crack down on them.

There is one thing that I do have to say about buffet people in general, though. After having traveled from buffet to buffet all across this great land of ours, I have discovered that buffet people are some of the friendliest people you'll ever find. They're also some of the most polite. Sometimes they'll even let you cut in line in front of them. Especially if you happen to have the last available chicken leg on your plate. Then, when you glance away from your plate just long enough to get a scoop of carrots . . . well, let's just say, all's fair in love, war, and buffet lines.

My doctor told me to stop having intimate
dinners for four.
Unless there are three other people.
—Orson Welles

Last Breaths and Country Music

The trouble with real life is that there's no danger music.
—Jim Carrey from *The Cable Guy*

Maybe the Cable Guy had it right. How much easier would life be for all of us if every time we started to do something that would end with dire consequences, danger music would begin to play, warning us of impending doom, just like it happens in the movies? Wouldn't it be much nicer if we knew what not to do, whom to stay away from, and when to duck?

It would help us, too, if we could have romantic music playing at all the right times. Husbands and wives wouldn't have to guess what kind of mood each other was in; the music would tell them. Even if her husband was passed out on the sofa, a wife would know by the beautiful music that's playing in the background that love is in the air, despite all the snoring.

My husband and I live in the Nashville area, the home of country music. I love most kinds of music, but I especially enjoy country music. You can't beat songs like "Dropkick Me, Jesus, Through the Goal Posts of Life" and "You're the Reason Our Kids Are So Ugly." I grew up with a father who played a lot of country and gospel music in our home. But country music, and even gospel, has evolved over the years, keeping up with the times and gathering a whole new generation of fans along the way.

There is one thing that I've always wondered about, especially when it comes to certain country ballads and cowboy songs. There seems to be a good number of these old songs that were written about dying, and according to the lyrics, these songs were written by the very one who was doing the dying. Does that sound strange to anyone else besides me? They're nice songs, don't get me wrong, but they do make you wonder how it is that these songs ever got written in the first place. Songwriting is hard enough to do when you're healthy and sitting at your computer or in a recording studio. But to write a song after you've just had a bullet go through you, now that takes amazing concentration, skill, and fortitude.

Let's look at the words of one old cowboy song called "The Dying Outlaw."

Come gather around me, my comrades and friends,
For the sun it is setting on life's short day;
For I'm wounded to die and there's nothing to do,
But wait 'til my life ebbs away.

Now, right there is my point. Here is this mortally wounded cowboy outlaw, lying in the dust breathing what could possibly be his last breath, but instead of asking for someone to go fetch the doc, or even a Band-Aid, he's penning a song lyric. I don't know if he's writing it in the dust, or if he dragged himself over to his horse and grabbed a pad of paper and a pencil out of his satchel. All I know is this poor bleeding cowboy gathered up all the strength he had left and said, "I may have lead in me, but I've got a song in me, too! Stand back and watch me create! By the way, does anyone know what rhymes with bullet?"

The poor guy isn't even going to be around to spend the royalty checks if the song is a hit, but he's not giving any thought to money or even himself. He's simply thinking of future generations of cowboy music lovers, and he's penning his final thoughts as he breathes his last few breaths. Obviously, he's a deadline writer. Music companies would have loved him.

"When do you think you'll have the song finished?"

"Well, I'll probably be dead by one, so say, noonish?"

Poor guy. If only he had realized his talent and passion for songwriting earlier, his life might have taken a different turn. He could have been wonderfully successful in the music industry and turned his back on his life of crime. Music might have even ended up saving his life—after all, deadlines do have a tendency to keep one going.

"We'd really like another verse. Can you hang on a little bit longer?"

"I dunno. I'm getting pretty weak. I'll try to get one more

verse out of me, but there's no way I can write a bridge, too."

From ballads to pop to rock to country to gospel, the whole world loves a good song. Some songs soothe us, others make us feel romantic. Some energize us, others make us feel sad and melancholy, while still others can make us feel like we're on top of the world.

For us middle-agers and beyond, songs can do something else, too. They can take us back to a simpler time, back to a point in our life before we had lived so much of it. A song can transport us back through time to our high school graduation, our wedding day, or any other special time in our lives. They can rekindle the passion in our marriage, the love for our fellow man, and even our feelings for our very first dog. Tell me, who among us can listen to "Old Shep" and not tear up?

Songs can also get us moving again. It's hard to listen to a song with a good beat and not feel like tapping your toes or clapping along. And if you've never tried doing housework or yardwork to music, you ought to give it a try. You'll be surprised at how much faster you move and how much more you get done.

Songs can fill our loneliness, too, and be our company. We don't feel quite so alone when there's music playing in our homes.

So whether it's love songs, ballads, inspiration songs, rock and roll, gospel, or the dying-cowboy ballad, the important thing is to be sure we're all getting plenty of music throughout our day. Like they say, music is the soul of life.

It's easy to play any musical instrument: all you have to do is touch the right key at the right time and the instrument will play itself.

—J. S. Bach

5

We B Bussin'

For my part, I travel not to go anywhere,
but to go. I travel for travel's sake.
The great affair is to move.
—Robert Louis Stevenson

With each year that passes, the idea of going on one of those bus tours sounds more and more inviting. You know the ones I'm talking about. They go to different tourist attractions like Washington, D.C., Orlando, the Smoky Mountains, Branson, and many other wonderful places. The most tempting part of these trips is the fact that you can just sit back and leave the driving to someone else. How nice is that? Sure, every once in a while a bus driver will fall asleep at the wheel and end up making his own off-ramp and landing in a ditch, but to my husband and me, even that seems like a small price to pay for not having to deal with rush-hour traffic in unfamiliar towns. Besides, who am I to complain? I've had my own fair share of automobile mishaps. While I've never fallen asleep at the wheel (napping at red lights doesn't count), I do have a tendency to back into objects, like cars, lampposts, trash cans, lawn mowers, and other assorted temporary and permanent objects. I figure that if I were still dragging around on my rear bumper everything that I have ever backed into, I would have a two-mile-long procession behind me.

Besides not having to drive in strange towns, there are other advantages to taking a tour bus. For one thing, if a tour bus driver gets lost, he or she won't hesitate to stop and ask for directions, or at the very least consult a map. Tour bus drivers know they're on a time schedule and that it's their responsibility to find out precisely where they are and how to get where they need to go. They won't drive around aimlessly for hours on end, telling themselves and their passengers that the right road is "just around the corner."

If a husband, on the other hand, happens to get lost, you will visit four extra states before he'll even think about stopping and asking for directions. *"I don't need no stinkin' map!"* he'll say as you pass the same street for the eighteenth time. The only thing he uses a map for is to keep the sun off the dash or to swat some mosquitoes.

Another advantage to taking a tour bus trip is that most buses have rest rooms on board. You don't have to beg, threaten, or hold the driver hostage to get him to make a rest room stop. All you have to do is get up and walk to the on-board facilities, which I'm happy to say don't usually have all the graffiti that some gas station rest rooms can have. What would one of these bus passengers write, anyway? "AARP RULES"?

What is it about husbands that they hate to pull over to a gas station for these pit stops? Were they scared by a gas station attendant in their formative years? Or are they afraid they'll be made fun of by all those other male drivers they passed along the road? To a man, there's nothing worse than making great time, passing car after car, motor home after motor home, eighteen wheeler after eighteen wheeler, only to find yourself stuck behind those very same vehicles once you get back on the road after your stop. The ridicule and embarrassment for this kind of loss of time and distance is far too much of a blow to a man's driving ego. It can cause a man to pull over and move to the backseat, curl up in the fetal position and whimper like a baby for the next hundred miles. It's a sad sight and it could very well be the whole reason why husbands won't stop. It's not that they don't love us and want to take care of our needs, it's just that they know all too well where it can lead. They also know that it will cause them to come in last in the secret road race among men, and they're not about to forfeit their chances of winning the coveted trophy. No one ever sees this trophy, of course. They have to keep it hidden, otherwise we'll catch on to them and the contest will be over.

And so, a bus tour is sounding better and better to me. Or maybe someday I'll even get a job driving one. I hear in Branson they've got tour buses that can double as boats and be driven straight into the lake. That sounds like fun, and since I've already been doing that for years with my own car, I might as well get paid for it.

> *My husband would go to the ends of the earth for me. But if he'd just stop and ask directions, he wouldn't have to.*
> —Martha Bolton

Ideal Destinations for the Menopausal Traveler

- Cool, California
- Briny Breezes, Florida
- Energy, Illinois
- Relief, Kentucky
- Pep, Texas
- Sweatman, Mississippi
- Waterproof, Louisiana
- Burning Well, Pennsylvania
- Dripping Springs, Texas
- Thermal, California
- Tightsqueeze, Virginia
- Wide Awake, Colorado
- Why, Arizona

Death by Fashion

Be not the first by whom the new are tried,
nor yet the last to lay the old aside.
—Alexander Pope

I almost killed myself once. I didn't try jumping off a bridge
or throwing myself in front of a speeding bus or anything like
that. No, the way I almost did myself in was with a pair of
tights. I wasn't depressed. I was just trying to be fashionable.
And since it was winter, I was also trying to keep warm. But
the tights were about two sizes too small (or I was two sizes
too big), and by the end of the day, they had cut off my circulation so much that the room was spinning and I was starting
to see glimpses of a tunnel of light.

I didn't actually want to die. It was just that I had purchased a pair of Petite tights by mistake, and I was trying to
avoid the embarrassment of having to take them back to the
store and ask for a larger size. So I went ahead and wore
them anyway.

But squeezing my Tall size body into a Petite size pair of
tights is a little like pouring a gallon of milk into a sippee cup:

No matter how carefully you pour, there's going to be plenty of overflow.

Tights aren't the only life-threatening item of clothing that I have encountered over my lifetime. I once had a pair of jeans whose zipper would periodically slide southward with no warning whatsoever, taking a souvenir clump of my skin along with it. Since I prefer all of my clumps of flesh to stay together, I decided to toss out the jeans.

But the most dangerous article of clothing ever designed has got to be the turtleneck. Not the flesh kind of turtleneck that inspired the title of this book. I'm talking about the real kind of turtleneck. Turtleneck as in "turtleneck sweater." If you ask me, the turtleneck should come with a warning. "The attempted removal of this product could be hazardous to your health . . . and dignity."

Let me explain. It was a day like any other day—I was shopping. Sweaters were on sale at this particular department store, and since winter was coming, I wanted to get a new one. I found a sweater I liked, a pretty red turtleneck, but they didn't have it in my size. The only one they had was two sizes too small, but since it was rather bulky, I convinced myself that I could still fit into it. And I did. Sort of. It took quite a bit of struggling, but there in the privacy of my dressing room, I somehow managed to get it on. It looked pretty good, too. So good, in fact, that I decided I was going to purchase it.

As soon as I started to take it off, though, things took a definite turn for the worse. Have you ever tried removing a two-sizes-too-small turtleneck sweater from your body? If you're still alive and reading this book, you probably haven't. For twenty minutes I struggled with that thing, only to get more and more tangled up in the process. I now know what a string of Christmas tree lights must feel like when you're trying to unravel them. I was withdrawing and inserting my arms and head into various holes, none of them the right one. I even ended up with one of my arms in the sleeve of another sweater that was hanging in the dressing room. If you ask me, the designer who first came up with the concept of the turtleneck sweater must have worked at Bellevue in the straitjacket department. For the life of me, I couldn't find my way out of that sweater! I looked like Houdini in an escape gone bad, and I was starting to hyperventilate with each twist and tug. I thought about calling the store security officer to help, but I didn't know how they handled their cases of "Turtleneck Assault."

Trying to maintain as much dignity as possible, I continued to wiggle and wrestle with the garment, but I was getting more and more entangled in the process. I stumbled out of the dressing room, still in the turtleneck of doom, and tried my best to flag down a store clerk, which was pretty easy to do considering the sleeves of the sweater were now dangling above my head, and when I moved back and forth in a rapid motion, they flapped in the breeze like a wind sock.

A clerk did finally come to my aid and helped me out of my predicament. She seemed to take it all in stride, too, which makes me wonder if this sort of thing happens to a lot of people when they try on turtlenecks.

I thanked her for releasing me from my entrapment, then

asked where the much safer cardigans were. She pointed to the next section over, but before I could walk over there, she made me sign a paper vowing to never trespass in the Petite section again. Since I had already signed a similar paper in the hosiery department, I willingly reached for the pen and signed it. I had been shamed enough—what was a little more humiliation? And anyway, staying out of the Petite section was for my own health and safety. As nice as it is to see a smaller size tag on an item of clothing that I happen to be wearing, I certainly don't want to require the Jaws of Life to be removed from it.

Clothing attacks such as the above are our own fault. In both instances I had tried on items that were not my correct size. But there are some situations where the fashion designers are at fault. How many times have they brought designs to the runways that were potentially lethal? Remember those blouses with long, flowing sleeves that came into fashion a few years ago? I bought several of them just to be in style, but I soon discovered that there was one little problem. Every time I cooked, they tended to catch on fire. My smoke alarm gets enough of a workout between my cooking and my hot flashes, so I don't need my blouses igniting and adding to the drama. I also didn't like how the sleeves tended to hang down past my jacket sleeves. I would try tucking them back up into the sleeve, but they would inevitably work their way out again and I would end up with what looked like propellers at the ends of each of my arms. I didn't care about the embarrassment. I was just afraid that I could take off in a gust of wind and no one would know it was the blouse's fault. For my own safety, and because I hate to fly, I had to give the blouses away.

Men have had to deal with dangerous fashions over the years, too. I wonder if anyone has ever done a survey to find out how many men have passed out from accidentally tying their necktie too tight? And bow ties? How safe can they be? Especially if you show up at a biker rally wearing one.

And whose idea was it to use straight pins to keep men's shirts folded neatly in their packages? I wonder how much blood has been spilled on the battleground of dressing rooms all over the world over this strange practice?

Dangerous fashions aren't anything new, though. The problem goes way back in our history. Ever heard of the hoopskirt? It's hard to believe that during the mid–1880s some designer was actually paid money for inventing this undergarment. Who knows how many women were knocked unconscious simply by trying to sit down in a hoopskirt. There aren't any records of injuries, but that's probably because the incidents were listed as "a severe attack of the vapors," when in reality it was hoopskirt assault. And where did the inventor of the hoopskirt come up with the idea any-way? While playing around with a couple of hoops one day, did he just throw some fabric over them and say to himself, *"Hmmm . . . now here's a style that will make a woman's lower half look even larger. Women are going to love this!"*?

Back then, there was also the corset. Now what kind of cruel mind was behind that insane fashion item? Corsets were such a tight squeeze on a lady that all sorts of body parts were being pushed into places where they didn't belong.

"Dahling, I can't help but notice that you have a hole in the vicinity of your throat. Did you have some sort of surgical procedure done?"

"Oh, goodness no, Abigail. That's just my belly button."

I'm glad someone finally wised up and we don't have to wear things like hoopskirts and corsets today. Can you imagine how long it would take to unfasten a corset at a buffet?

The Roaring '20s had its share of dangerous fashion, too. There was all that fringe and beads; and as if that new look wasn't dangerous enough, someone decided to make up the Charleston dance. I wonder how many women accidentally beat themselves to death doing the Charleston in those beaded dresses during that era?

What is wrong with us? Why do we consistently pay these fashion designers our hard-earned money only to have them come up with styles that have the potential to harm us? And who are these people, anyway? It used to be that most of the top fashion designers could be found living in Paris or New York. But I don't think that's the case anymore. If you ask me, they're all working at Goodwill now. That's right, Goodwill Industries. Maybe they're not on the payroll, but they're hanging out there, I'm sure of it. Think about it. Every time you go through your closet and finally give away all of your outdated clothing, what's the next hot style to hit the market? That's right—the very style you just gave away. So it stands to reason that someone on the inside track at Goodwill is going through these donations and bringing these fashions back into style as soon as you drop them off. The timing is far too perfect for it to be a mere coincidence.

You can try waiting out the designers, but it usually doesn't work. I know this from personal experience. I've held out year after year, passing on the donation for just a little bit longer, giving this shirt, those pants, that skirt one more season to see if the style was going to come back on its own, but it didn't. At least not until I actually took the outdated clothes off their hangers, placed them in a bag, and drove them over to a Goodwill donation center. Not until then did those looks ever start showing up on store mannequins again.

You can check out my theory for yourself, but I believe you'll find my thinking is right on. If anyone goes through their attic and gives away an old hoopskirt and corset, we're all in trouble.

The novelties of one generation are only the resuscitated fashions of the generation before last.
—George Bernard Shaw

Is There a Doctor in the House?

Never go to a doctor whose office plants have died.
—Erma Bombeck

Thanks to recent advances in medical technology, as well as an effort to keep expenses down for the patient, more and more surgical procedures are now being performed in doctors' offices instead of in a hospital.

Now, anything that will reduce the soaring cost of medical care is probably a good thing, but caution is still recommended. I recently read an article that said in some states, health boards are not required to regulate doctors' offices as vigorously as they would a hospital setting. If this is true, should something go wrong during the procedure, a patient's well-being could be jeopardized if the doctor's staff are not adequately trained or prepared, or if the office lacks the necessary equipment to handle the crisis.

While most doctors probably do their best to meet the government's standards, I'm sure there are some doctors' offices where caution would be highly suggested. Because of this, I thought it might be a good idea to issue the following warning as a public service:

Do not allow your doctor to operate on you in his office if . . .

- any of the surgical tools have the words "The Home Depot" printed on them.
- he has to clear off his copy machine to make an operating table.
- his procedure room has a drive-thru.
- his anesthesiologist is holding a hammer.
- his oxygen mask says "Property of American Airlines."
- anywhere on his medical license you see the words "For entertainment value only."
- everyone in his waiting room is a malpractice attorney.
- his EKG machine has only two knobs and the words "Etch A Sketch."
- his defibrillator is a fork and an electric outlet.
- you hear the word "oops" more than three times—and he's just trying to cut through the surgical supplies packaging.

It's good to save money, especially in the increasingly costly field of medical care. But it's up to us to make sure that the care we are receiving is the best care available. Take time to ask whether or not your doctor's office is properly prepared should an emergency arise during any in-office surgical procedure. After all, your body is the only one you're going to get. It's just one to a customer, and it has to last you a long time, so take the best care of it you can.

Medical Definitions for the Middle-Aged Patient and Beyond

As you move through the middle-age years and beyond, it's a good idea to keep up with the latest medical terms. Should your doctor refer to any of the following on your medical report, you want to be in the know. The following list is provided for this purpose:

Fibrillation— not confessing to your doctor about the four chili dogs you had just before the chest pain began

Anti-inflammatory— not wanting to argue with your doctor over a billing error

Bronchospasm— leg cramps after a day of horseback riding with your grandchildren

Atrophy—	what you win in the Baby Boomer Bowling League
Microcirculation—	not meeting many people at the retirement home Christmas party
Serological—	eating sensible cereal
Carbohydrate—	drinking bottled water in your car
Thermoregulation—	asking your spouse to get you a second blanket
Arrhythmogenic—	the urge to dance in a sterile environment
Gastralgia—	that nauseous feeling you get when looking at the price of gasoline
Benign—	a possible winning number in a game of bingo at the seniors' center
Lower GI—	a low-ranking member of the military
CAT Scan—	looking for the jazz station on your radio

They had me on the operating table all day.
They looked into my stomach, my gall bladder,
they examined everything inside of me.
Know what they decided? I need glasses.
—Joe E. Lewis

10

New Prescription Medicines for Middle-Aged Patients*

Fanthropan: Provides immediate relief from menopausal hot flashes. Open box, discard medication, then wave the "Possible Side Effects" insert in front of face until hot flash subsides.

Silencithor: Insert one pill into each ear one hour prior to grandchild's birthday party. Provides temporary deafness for up to three hours for one dozen four-year-olds. Silencithor PM is double the size and strength. When inserted into ears it can block out spousal snoring of up to twenty-one decibels.

Lazichor: Take one dosage every morning for eight-hour relief from wife's honey-do nagging. Induces temporary but instant comalike state. Works best if taken in recliner in front of television set.

Golficillin: One tablet taken one hour prior to tee time provides invisibility for up to ten minutes, which for most adult male patients is just enough time to make it out of the house with your golf clubs.

Memorazine: For memory enhancement. Take one every morning to remember what other pills you're supposed to be taking. Will also work to enhance memory for when you walk into a room but can't remember why you walked into the room in the first place.

Summersporin: Two drops in each eye will temporarily dim vision for up to two hours per dosage during swimsuit shopping season. Works best if administered ten minutes before entering dressing room.

*Check with your doctor to see if these new medications are right for you.

11

What Are They Doing Now?

Retirement at sixty-five is ridiculous.
When I was sixty-five I still had pimples.
—George Burns

Retirement doesn't mean you're dead. It just means you don't have to look alive unless you want to. You can sleep until noon, then laze around on the sofa the rest of the day if you so choose. You can stay in your robe and slippers until supper. Or even next summer. You don't have to shave your face or your legs (whichever applies) for weeks. Maybe even months. Men can look like ZZ Top if they want to and women can grow bangs on their knees if they so choose. It's their choice. Retirement means you are master of your own ship and hair follicles. You can chart an independent course.

As a retiree, whatever you do and wherever you go is strictly up to you. No matter how many people you've worked for in your lifetime, you are your own boss now—

theoretically speaking, of course. You may still have your spouse to answer to, and perhaps a couple of precocious two-year-old grandchildren. But as far as having to get up in the morning and report to work, that's a thing of the past. You can toss out your alarm clock and never have to answer your beeper or work cell phone again.

Ah, yes, retirement is wonderful. The freedom, the peace, the quiet, the sleeping in, the naps, the independence . . . that is, until you take that first post-retirement job. And many retirees do exactly that. Research tells us that it's healthy to stay busy and to keep one's mind active after retirement.

Second careers are also the perfect opportunity for you to try something different and learn new skills. If you retired from a high-stress job, you might prefer spending your middle-aged years working in a far more relaxed atmosphere. If you spent twenty or thirty years working in a, how shall we say it, *boring* industry, then you might be ready for a little more excitement this time around.

After my husband retired from the Los Angeles Police Department (three times, to be exact—I believe he holds the record), and after working for a period of time as Security Manager for one of the major television studios, he didn't want any job where high levels of stress were involved. He had seen enough tense situations to last him a lifetime.

So his dream job became operating the train at Knott's Berry Farm. Not that there is anything wrong with being a train conductor at an amusement park. I'm sure it's a job that requires a good amount of skill. Dodging park guests has to be tricky, especially when they are crossing the tracks with an armful of giant stuffed animals and balloons blocking their line of vision.

I think the main reason my husband wanted to be an amusement park train conductor is that he thought it would be cool to pull the cord and sound the whistle. I offered to have a cord and whistle installed in our SUV, one that he could pull whenever he drove up our driveway, but he didn't seem to think it would be the same. (So apparently, it wasn't only the whistle. It must have been the uniform, too.)

Whatever his reasoning, his dream job never came to fruition. We moved to Tennessee and commuting to Buena Park, California, wasn't really an option.

In Tennessee, though, he ended up taking a job at the Opryland Hotel. It wasn't operating a train, but it was close. It was operating the boats that take the tourists down a canal that runs through the hotel. The uniforms were khaki, and not as cool in his opinion as a train conductor's uniform, but all in all he did enjoy that job. He was glad he didn't have to carry a gun (goldfish don't get all that violent), and there weren't any muggings to have to deal with on that canal either. That's probably because a mugger would have had to snatch the purse or wallet, dive overboard, then swim through a treacherous two feet of raging—okay, rippling water to make his escape, and do it all while listening to "Achy Breaky Heart" over the speaker system. Apparently no mugger wanted to put their lives in that much jeopardy. Besides, any assailant would have been quickly overtaken by busloads of vacationing tourists, and we all know how quickly they can turn into vigilantes when someone threatens their enjoyment of a lobby boat ride.

Even without the danger and prestige of the train conductor job, the Opryland job still ended up going to my husband's head. He began making me and our children address him as "Admiral," and all night long he would make us listen to his tales of harrowing adventures while commanding his "fleet of ships."

But as beautiful as the setting was (and the Opryland Hotel is amazing), even he needed a little more excitement than a lobby boat ride. So he began thinking about reentering the security field.

He is now Chief of Security of an art museum, which is not only a peaceful and beautiful place to work, but it also makes better use of his police and security skills. Finally, a perfect fit.

Finding that ideal second career isn't always an easy thing to do. Unfortunately, society is too often geared toward younger and younger workers. But that rationale doesn't make much sense to me. Why would a company overlook the already proven qualities that a seasoned middle-ager can bring to the table? Twenty-year-olds just don't have the same experience and sound judgment of an older worker. Middle-agers aren't going to use the company Internet for video games or demand special parking for their skateboards. But too often companies don't see these obvious advantages, and they overlook quality for youth, time and time again.

I'm sure we all know highly skilled individuals who have been looking for that perfect second career for years, but with no luck. From retired teachers to retired entertainers to retired CEOs, there's a wealth of knowledge and talent out there in middle-aged land sitting dormant. It's a shame to continue to let the skills and experience of so many individuals go unused simply because they've passed the halfway mark of life. The business world needs to get busy and tap into this well of dormant but still very impressive talent and knowledge. Wal-Mart greeters, as good of a job as that might very well be, shouldn't be the only choice for these dedicated and capable workers. Age and experience is a plus, not a negative. Employers could reap the benefits of some other employer's years of training and save themselves money and problems in the long run.

If you're one of the ones who is currently looking for a second career, I would encourage you to not give up. Don't buy into the notion that your skills are no longer marketable. There are plenty of people who have made their greatest impact on society during the second half of their lives—Colonel Sanders, Grandma Moses, Ronald Reagan, Jimmy Carter, just to name a few. Just keep looking. That perfect opportunity is bound to come along one day. It did for my husband. He loves where he works now. It's the perfect fit he had been looking for after nearly three decades of police work. And don't think for a minute that his position at an art museum doesn't still carry a significant degree of danger, too. Why, one night during the holidays, the Lionel electric train in the Christmas display jumped the tracks, and he had to rise to the occasion once again. As he tells it, *"What else could I do? When the call came in, 'Train down,' I looked at my men and* said, 'I'm going in. Cover me, boys. I'm going in.'"

And the city (and electric-train lovers everywhere) sleeps in peace tonight.

Years may wrinkle the skin, but to give up enthusiasm wrinkles the soul.
—Samuel Ullman

12

Computer Signs for the Middle-Ager and Beyond

S :) = "So how do you like my new toupee?"

/ :) = "Can you tell I've got a comb over?"

{ } = "I don't remember these love handles being so prominent before."

: - x = "Who needs to count carbs when you've got duct tape?"

}} — I = "Drat! My forehead's in my eyes again."

:B - (= "Is it just me or are the bags under my eyes getting worse?"

: - ()　　=　"I just had Botox. Can you tell?"

8 -)　　=　"Has anyone seen my glasses? I've been looking for them for the last—Oh, silly me. They're on my face."

X :)　　=　"Fred, take the propeller hat off and act your age!"

W
. .
—　　　=　"I know they're only four hairs, but do what you can with them."
///
. .
O　　　=　"What do you mean the air-conditioner's broken?"

13

Gravity
(Parody of "Yesterday")

Gravity
Wish this wasn't how things had to be.
Body parts are falling off of me.
Oh, why did God make gravity?
Can you see
how my figure has dropped to my knees?
Not much else is where it used to be
since I lost out to gravity.
Why can't things just stay where God put them long ago?
All day long I'm warning folks to "Look out below!"
Gravity
I've been shrinking, now I'm half of me.
I might not stop until I'm four foot three.
Oh, why did God make gravity?

Let's Leave My Brain Out of This

Americans are getting stronger. Twenty years ago, it took two people to carry ten dollars worth of groceries. Today, a five-year-old can do it.
—Henny Youngman

I recently read about a new marketing concept called "neuromarketing." Instead of merely taking our word on our opinions, companies will soon be able to use neuroimaging to determine whether our brains are backing up what our mouths are saying about their products. It's sort of like being hooked up to a lie-detector test for the Pepsi/Coke challenge. Companies want to be sure that when we say we like their products, we really *do* like their products. They don't want nice and polite. They want truth. Only honest to goodness feedback can help grow their business. Considering the advantages of such advanced technology, I'm sure there will be plenty of companies signing up for neuromarketing programs.

But has anyone thought about what could happen if the technology behind neuromarketing were to go beyond product analysis and become available to the general public? The ramifications could be enormous. Telephone solicitors would have to tell you the truth about that pyramid scheme they're pitching to you over the phone. And if you told them you were in the middle of dinner and couldn't talk right now, they would know by the neuroimaging whether or not you were telling the truth. When that waitress asks how your lunch is, instead of getting away with a simple but insincere "Fine," she would be able to read your brain and immediately know about all that gristle you're hiding under the parsley. And just imagine how quickly neuroimaging would reveal false friends and mother-in-law/son-in-law relationships. Yes, if this technology were available to the general public, there's no telling what kinds of changes it would make to our lives.

It would even affect marriage. There would be no more forgotten birthdays, anniversaries, or Christmas gifts because absolutely no excuse would get by the neuroimager. The only thing a husband or wife could say is the truth. "I forgot." Simple as that.

Politics would be affected, too. Imagine the next presidential debate with neuromarketing in action. One candidate might begin with, "With all due respect to my esteemed opponent," while the neuroimagining is indicating that what he's really saying is, *There's no way this doofus could run the country!*" (A few go ahead and say that now anyway.)

The technology wouldn't really be necessary on those of us over forty, though. By the time we've reached this age, most of us can't wait to share our true feelings. We've held our opinions in long enough. We realize life is much too short to mince words or beat around the bush. If we don't like a product, or if we think there is a better way to make it, we'll usually let the company know about it. We'll call and speak directly to the department head. We'll write letters to the corporate office. We'll tell our neighbors and friends. We'll share our opinions with anyone who'll listen. But by the same token, if we're impressed with a product, we're just as quick to let the company know about that, too. Middle-agers and beyond are a marketing team's dream.

Until the rest of the population can catch up on the sincerity of the middle-aged shopper, though, companies are going to have to depend on new techniques like neuro-marketing to do their research. After all, it's only through getting the honest opinion of their customers, young and old alike, that companies will be able to give us the products we truly want and can actually use.

And as far as neuroimaging's effect on mother-in-law/son-in-law relationships, well, sometimes it's best to just leave well enough alone.

My opinions may have changed, but not the fact that I am right.
—Ashleigh Brilliant

15

I Hereby Bequeath

**Death is not the end. There remains the
litigation over the estate.**
—Ambrose Bierce

There is a fear worse than knowing your children and grand-children will fight over all your possessions after your passing. And that is, *What if they don't?* What if all those souvenir trinkets you've carted around from house to house, all that stuff you couldn't bear to part with, all the pictures, furniture, books, dishes, rugs, and all the rest are set to be sold to the highest bidder as soon as you take your final breath? What if your family already has the garage sale signs printed up and they're just waiting to fill in the date? What if not one of your offspring is interested in hanging on to your hot-dog-shaped condiment tray? What if no one wants your elephant statue or your pink flamingo lamp? What if they can't wait to get rid of your Lone Ranger video series? What if no one wants your "stuff"?

No matter how many priceless treasures we've accumu-lated over the years, no matter how neatly we've displayed them, or how protective we have been of every single cherished item, in the end there is only one thing that we can do with any of it, and that's leave it behind. We can't take a single Tony Bennett album with us. We don't even get a two-suitcase allowance on our flight to eternity. We have to go out the same way we came in, empty-handed. All we can take with us is what is inside of us. It's like that old joke about never seeing a hearse towing a U-Haul trailer. No matter how much we might love our stuff, not one single item is making the trip to the hereafter with us. It's all staying behind, and it'll be up to those we leave behind to do with it as they so choose.

So maybe it's time to rip the protective plastic coverings off our sofas and start enjoying them in the here and now. Maybe it's time to start getting some use out of our priceless collectibles, instead of merely watching them accumulate dust. Maybe we should start building some memories of those things that we've been keeping up on our shelves. After all, a "keepsake" won't mean anything to your family unless there are some actual memories attached to it.

Going ahead and giving away a few of your things while you're still healthy might be a good idea, too. It helps us make sure we're giving the right mementos to the right people, and that we're not tossing out those things that mean the most to our families and hanging on to those things that mean the least. Too often we have no idea which items in our homes are most cherished by our children until they tell us years later that they would have liked that overstuffed chair we gave away for free to some stranger.

I'm not sure which of our things my children will want after my husband and I are no longer around. I hope they don't hold the mother of all garage sales and sell for mere pennies item after item, totally unaware of their real value. (The hot-dog-shaped condiment tray alone is number 346 of 1,000,000,000 and should be worth something.).

Like all of us who get to this point in life, I hope there are plenty of things around our house that do hold some special meaning to our children, regardless of any monetary value. Things that will bring to their minds heartwarming memories every time they look at them. Maybe it'll be the Christmas decorations (I am a certifiable Christmas fanatic), or the old photo albums (I am a picture junkie), or our book collection (both their father and I have a book collection that would rival the Library of Congress). Whatever items hold special memories for our children, I hope they'll recall those memories every time they see them.

If you are going to start giving away your things early, though, there is something to keep in mind. Don't give away those things that still give you pleasure. They're yours. You don't have to part with them until you're good and ready. Only give away those things that will give you greater pleasure watching someone else enjoy them for a while.

You might want to donate some of your possessions to a museum, church, or charity. Or you might even hold that mother of all garage sales yourself and take the money and go on a cruise. We've all seen estate sales of people who had died penniless, depressed, and all alone while they hung on to a houseful of possessions that weren't doing them any good at all. Possessions that were all too quickly sold to the highest bidder, raising a small fortune for the heirs, who had never taken the time to visit the deceased anyway.

It's like the old joke about an elderly man who, after many years of his family's complaining about his inability to hear, finally went out and bought himself a hearing aid. After wearing it for a few weeks, he went back to the doctor for a routine checkup. The doctor said, "Your hearing is perfect. It couldn't be better. I bet your family's pretty thrilled that you're hearing again, huh?" The man said, "My family? Are you kidding? I haven't told any of them yet. I just hang out in my recliner and listen to their conversations. I've changed my will three times!"

Junk or treasure, useless or collectible, the bottom line is they're your things. Keep them, give them away, do with them what you will. Then go about the business of enjoying your life.

I'm very proud of my gold pocket watch. My grandfather, on his deathbed, sold me this watch.
—Woody Allen

16

Today's Weather for the Menopausal Woman

Heat wave to continue, with intermittent volatility; some storms may be severe. An 80 percent chance of flash flooding, mostly indoors, during the overnight hours.

17

The Face-Lift-of-the-Month Club

I wish I had a twin, so I could know what I'd look like without plastic surgery.
—Joan Rivers

Television reality shows and magazine ads try to convince us that plastic surgery will give us back our youth and vitality, that it will put everything back in place and fix what may have needed fixing all along, that it is the answer to all our problems. But even though plastic surgery has become more routine and is helping more and more people look younger and younger, there is one other danger that plastic surgery candidates should be aware of. It's not always easy to know when to quit.

We have all seen those celebrities who seem to have a frequent-user pass for plastic surgery. Those stars who seem to spend so much time at their plastic surgeon's office, they get their fan mail there. The ones who are getting this nipped and that tucked and eventually end up looking like something out of a wax museum.

Some of these youth-seeking stars have had so much work done, their facial muscles don't even operate correctly anymore. They think they're smiling, but nothing on their face has moved to indicate that. They frown, but no one knows it. Their face is stuck with one expression, and it's like talking to a photograph.

After the sixth or seventh plastic surgery, you would think that friends and family of these desperate folks would try to arrange some sort of plastic surgery intervention.

"You've got to stop this, Beulah! Look what you're doing to yourself! Every time you blow your nose, it flies right off and you've got to spend twenty minutes looking for it. One of these days you're not going to be able to get it to stick back on. Stop this madness before it's too late!"

But these people don't stop. And thanks to the "makeover" reality shows, more people are getting plastic surgery than ever before. Men and women are lining up for every body part renovation you can think of, and now they're wanting to do it in package deals. They want their face lifted, their thighs liposuctioned, their chin reshaped, their teeth capped, their hair transplanted, and various other body parts enlarged, reduced, rearranged, and rejuvenated all during the same leave of absence from work. I guess they figure if *Trading Spaces* can give a room a complete makeover in two days, why can't a body remodel get done in the same amount of time?

But we're talking surgery here. There are health issues

that have to be taken into consideration. Sure, some of these televised body makeovers have been truly amazing, but we need to be careful that we're not just concentrating on the outside person, and forgetting about the remodeling job that often needs to take place on the inside.

If you're going to change something about your body, you need to be sure you're doing it for the right person—you. If you're happy with the way you look, that's all that matters. No one else's opinion counts.

If you're not happy and you do want to surgically change something about your body, then the best advice we can give you is to seek out the very best medical care you can find.

And know when to quit.

I recently watched one of those plastic surgery shows where a lady was having her lips redone because apparently they had gotten all lumpy from too many collagen injections. I guess I don't blame her for wanting the lumps out. After all, who wants lumpy lips? But why didn't someone stop her long before that point? Didn't they notice she was getting a little carried away? I don't think anyone is going for the lumpy lip or wax museum face on purpose. Some of these people have, to borrow Phyllis Diller's great line, had "more parts lifted than an abandoned Mercedes." They don't even look like themselves anymore. They've turned into a montage of coveted body parts of every celebrity they've ever admired. They got the nose of this star, the lips of that star, and the chin of someone else. They have so many mismatched parts, their driver's license photo could pass for a Picasso painting.

Some years ago a friend of mine underwent plastic surgery to have a bump removed from her nose. The surgery was successful in that she got the nose she'd always dreamed of. But a short time after the surgery her now perfectly bumpless nose began pulling to the right. I don't think it was a political statement or anything, it was just doing it for no apparent reason.

With each passing week her nose would slide farther and farther off center. In a weird sort of way, her nose had become a sort of nomad, traveling the surface of her face, and there was nothing that she could do about it short of another surgery. The nose finally came to rest so close to the side of her face, it gave new meaning to the term, "Blow it out your ear!"

She did eventually have the second surgery and it all turned out fine. But getting to that point was a long and embarrassing process. For a couple of years her Christmas card photos looked like Mrs. Potato Head. Each year's card showed her nose in a different place on her face.

It's because of stories like this that I've decided to keep my less-than-perfect body just the way it is. I'm happy with it, flaws and all. I don't really have any problem with anyone else getting plastic surgery. It's their choice. But for me for right now, I'm sticking with what I've got. Besides, whenever I need to blow my nose, I kinda like knowing where to find it.

I think your whole life shows in your face and you should be proud of that.

—Lauren Bacall

Top 20 Countdown for Middle-Agers and Beyond

20. "Stumbling in the Night" (Frank Sinatra)
19. "You Can't Hurry Me" (Diana Ross and the Supremes)
18. "Everything Goes" (Tony Bennett)
17. "Whole Lotta Sweatin' Goin' On" (Jerry Lee Lewis)
16. "These Orthopedic Boots Are Made for Walking" (Nancy Sinatra)
15. "Listen to the Rhythm of the EKG" (The Cascades)
14. "Eve of Reconstruction" (Barry McGuire)
13. "You've Lost That Nerve End Feeling" (The Righteous Brothers)
12. "Papa's Got a Brand New Spleen" (James Brown)
11. "Stairway to Arrhythmia" (Neil Sedaka)
10. "It Hurts to Be This Age" (Gene Pitney)
 9. "Blue Suede Sensible Shoes" (Elvis)
 8. "Catch A Falling Part" (Perry Como)

7. "Ache Around the Clock" (Bill Haley and His Comets)
6. "Where Did My Teeth Go?" (Diana Ross and the Supremes)
5. "It's My Bypass and I'll Cry If I Want To" (Lesley Gore)
4. "Where Has All the Firmness Gone?" (Pete Seeger)
3. "Harper Valley AARP" (Jeannie C. Riley)
2. "Splenda, Splenda" (The Archies)
1. "Bridge Over Night-Sweat Puddles" (Simon and Garfunkel)

Middle-Age Evolution

My life has a superb cast but I can't figure out the plot.
—Ashleigh Brilliant

I don't believe in evolution. I don't believe that man started out as a monkey, then continued to evolve until he could fit into a decent business suit. It just doesn't make sense to me. I do, however, believe in a form of reverse evolution. In other words, after decades of dealing with everything that life has to throw at him, man can certainly go from perfect posture in his twenties and thirties, to looking rather apelike by his forties, fifties, and beyond. For me, this "reverse evolution" makes far more sense than the evolution chart. I'll show you what I mean.

Man at marriage ceremony: head erect, shoulders back, perfect posture.

Man after one weekend of carrying around honey-do list:

hunched over shoulders, head leaning slightly forward.

Man after birth of first child: hunched over shoulders, droopy eyes, unshaven face, head leaning forward.

Man on second week of mother-in-law's visit: hunched over shoulders, head noticeably lowered, arms dragging floor, face and neck with seven-day growth, communicates with grunting sounds.

Man after birth of fourth child: hunched over shoulders, head bouncing back and forth uncontrollably, scratches backside and under armpit seemingly without control, grunts to self, bears a slight animal-like odor (also resembles the scent of soiled diapers and spoiled milk).

Man after five hours of outlet shopping: hunched over shoulders, chin touching chest, massive overgrowth on face, neck, and back that could use a good mowing, makes apelike movements as he drags packages from store to store for life mate.

Man on third day of babysitting grandchildren: hunched over shoulders, head and chest have both succumbed to the gravitational pull, hasn't shaved in so long that hair has taken over and is now even growing out his ears.

Man after seeing how much his retirement check really is after retiring: hunched over shoulders, head dragging the floor, swings from workout equipment at YMCA in a futile attempt to try to take his mind off his situation.

Man holding stack of relationship books that his wife wants him to read: hunched over shoulders and lowered head, suddenly appears to not understand a word of English.

He shakes his head "no" in an apelike fashion, jumping up and down on the books.

Man after three hours of searching for lost television remote control: extremely hunched over shoulders, chin dragging on the ground, arms swinging from side to side, hairy and unkempt appearance, makes loud grunting noises, will clumsily knock over furniture in attempt to find remote. If lost item is not found, subject is likely to sit in a corner, picking things out of his navel, and pine away for hours.

By this point, man has indeed become a full-blown primate.

My wife has a slight impediment in her speech. Every now and then she stops to breathe.
—Jimmy Durante

Growing My Own Turtleneck

Some people try to turn back their odometers.
Not me, I want people to know why I look this
way. I've traveled a long way and some of the
roads weren't paved.
—Will Rogers

Some years ago while shopping at a local mall, I happened to catch a glimpse of myself in a mirror. That was when I first saw it. The Gathering. Skin Falls. Whatever you want to call it, all I know is somehow, some way, for some reason unbeknownst to me, I had managed to grow my own turtleneck.

It didn't matter how hard I tried not to look at it, there was no denying it. It was right there under my chin, plain as day. Where all that extra skin was coming from, I didn't have a clue. There was enough for a whole other person, maybe even a whole village, and some of it wasn't even my skin tone. But it was my skin nonetheless, and it was very much connected to me. Not tightly, but it was connected.

Sure, it was nice to know there was now enough skin there to keep me warm in the wintertime, but instinctively I knew there had to be some drawbacks. For one thing, I was now going to have to start rolling up my chin every time I ate soup.

Exactly where this flesh waterfall was originating from, I didn't have a clue. Layers and layers of what used to be taut, youthful skin had without warning started cascading down like a flesh-colored Niagara Falls.

As far as I could tell, this extra skin wasn't being pulled from other parts of my body. I regularly take inventory of my body (this is just something you do in middle age; the gravitational pull has a habit of relocating body parts on a regular basis, so I've found it's best to keep a log), but I couldn't find a gap anywhere. All of my original skin was present and accounted for. I had epidermis covering everything epidermis is supposed to be covering. Not one single internal organ was exposed. There was just a lot more skin than I had ever remembered having. It was like it had multiplied. And like I said, much of it had gathered under my neck.

So to this day, my "chin skirt," for lack of a better term, is still here and, short of surgery or duct tape, there isn't much I can do about it. I have, therefore, determined that since this book has now hit the bookstores and I've been able to spill my innermost feelings on the subject to you, my closest friends, I am not going to lose any more sleep over the issue. Why should I spend the rest of my life obsessing over changes that my body didn't even consult with me about? It's making these changes all on its own. All I can do is accept them and go on with my life.

According to some facial cream ads, the loosening of once perfectly fitting skin generally starts happening around forty years of age. For some of us, it might begin even sooner. If you've already experienced it, then you and I can commiserate together. If you haven't experienced it yet, count your blessings, but be assured the clock is ticking, and Chin Falls will eventually catch up to you. No one is immune.

Heredity and environmental factors have a lot to do with the degree of loosening that each person's skin might end up doing, but the bottom line is that at some point in our lives, we all have a date with gravity.

So learn from me. I, too, had taken my youthful, taut skin for granted. Every time I looked in the mirror, I counted on it being there. It had always been there before, a perfect fit. Until that one day in the mall when I was faced with the hard, cold, loose facts. My skin had let me down. It had let itself down. And it has been heading in that direction ever since.

My main complaint about all of this isn't so much the loose skin under my chin and elsewhere, but that all of this loosening took place without any warning whatsoever. It would have been nice to have had a warning. Why couldn't our bodies have come equipped with an alarm that would sound whenever these sorts of things are getting ready to take place, you know, like a tornado alert or a winter snowstorm advisory?

"Beep! Beep! Beep! Skin avalanche! Take cover immediately!"

Sure, it might get on people's nerves, like cell phones and car alarms do now, but at least we would have a warning for these sorts of bodily changes. And those standing near us would have the chance to take cover, too.

But there is no alarm system, so we'll just have to be on guard and take our changes as they come. And realize that the best defense against the downside of aging is a sense of humor.

There is still no cure for the common birthday.
—John Glenn

Season's Greetings

The earth has music for those who listen.
—William Shakespeare

By the time you've reached middle age, you have no doubt celebrated, dreaded, enjoyed, and endured your share of holiday seasons. The holidays take on a whole new look, sound, and feel for those of us in the over-forty crowd, especially when it comes to holiday music. Christmas carols can undergo quite a change when they're adjusted for the middle-ager. Instead of the more traditional songs that we're all used to hearing, carols like "I'm Beginning to Look a Lot Like Grandma," "The Twelve Days of Ointment," and "Oatmeal Roasting On An Open Fire" start filling our homes and hearts. "All I Want For Christmas Is Some Estrogen" is another favorite, too. Even a new version of "Here Comes Santa Claus" can be heard in the malls, especially in stores like the menopausal version of Victoria's Secret, Victoria's Who Cares?

Here comes menopause, here comes menopause,
right down Menopause Lane.
All wet with night sweats
and hot flashes, too,
it's like our bodies rain!
Moods are swinging, clothes are clinging,
we're puffin' up like a bun.
Pack the quilt before we wilt
'cause menopause has begun!

It's not just Christmas carols that are getting rewritten for those of us in the over-forty crowd. Our Valentine's Day music is different, too. Instead of sitting in front of the fireplace listening to the usual romantic fare, you'll find us listening to songs like "Achy Breaky Bones," "Hunka Hunka Burnin' Me," "You Don't Bring Me Rolaids Anymore," and "I Just Called to Say . . . I Can't Remember."

Our Fourth of Julys are sounding different, too. Come to one of our barbeques and you might hear "Praise the Lord and Pass the Metamucil" or that ol' patriotic favorite "Let Eardrums Ring."

And we can't forget New Year's Eve:

Should old acquaintance be forgot
and never brought to mind?
Or should we take our ginseng now
to help with auld lang syne?

Life seems to go on without effort, when I am filled with music.
—George Eliot

98

Life in Reality

**Life is not a problem to be solved, but a reality
to be experienced.**
—Søren Kierkegaard

Reality shows are all fine and good, but if the producers are looking for real heroism and adventure, they've missed the biggest angle yet. Surviving the Australian outback or some deserted, bug-infested island is nothing compared to what I have in mind. So what's my show?

Menopause House.

Think about it. It's the perfect reality show. The idea is to take ten menopausal women and put them in a trailer in the hot Nevada desert and make them live together without air-conditioning for two weeks. The last survivor would win a million dollars and a lifetime supply of estrogen. Right now I'm sure you're sitting there saying to yourself, *"Of course! Why didn't I think of that!"* It doesn't take much television savvy to realize this is an instant hit just waiting to happen. Interested producers may feel free to contact me through my Web site at *www.marthabolton.com,* or better yet, they can just send me the estrogen to option the rights to it.

The main drawback on a show like this would be the insurance; it would no doubt be astronomical (there's no telling what kind of antics ten estrogen-deprived, mood-swinging, hot-flashing, crowded, cranky women could pull). But it would be a fun show to watch, wouldn't it? At least from the safety of your living room. And talk about suspense—viewers would never know who was going to go off at any given moment. Any one of them could start a menopausal rant, and the best part is there wouldn't even need to be an inciting incident. Nothing would have to be staged or instigated. The sparks would be flying for absolutely no reason at all. Throw in the fact that there's no air-conditioning and you have a potential hostage situation brewing.

Besides insurance, another major expense of the show would be tissue. *Menopause House* would be full of emotional moments. With ten menopausal women talking about their lives, their day, their bowl of cornflakes that just went soggy, why, the weeping could go on for days. But that's okay; the desert's used to flash floods.

And then there's the whole claustrophobia thing. What hot-flashing woman could bear to maneuver her way down the hallway of a trailer with nine other menopausal women trying to do the same thing? That many hot flashes happening simultaneously could not only set the trailer ablaze, but it could possibly set off a range fire, the likes of which no cowboy has ever seen.

So like I said, I'm just waiting for the television networks to contact me. I have a strong feeling this could be next season's big hit. That is, if the public is brave enough for it.

I find television very educating. Every time somebody turns on the set, I go into the other room and read a book.
—Groucho Marx

The Older We Get

The older we get, the more we realize that money, while certainly nice to have, is far from being everything.

The older we get, the more we appreciate our time- and crisis-tested friends. Unless you're a jogger, who needs friends who run?

The older we get, the more skeptical we become of the news and gossip. We've lived long enough to know that there are always two sides to a story. We also know that there is a lot more positive news out there than what they are telling us.

The older we get, the more we know that failure isn't permanent.

The older we get, the more we realize that the things we stress over are very seldom worth stressing over.

The older we get, the more we appreciate good days, even if they weren't quite as good as we're recalling them.

The older we get, the more we value our money and appreciate the good it can do.

The older we get, the more we want to mean something significant to someone.

The older we get, the more we realize that our time is far too valuable to waste.

The older we get, the more we know the healing power of laughter.

The Grandmother of Invention

An amazing invention—but who would ever want to use one?
—Rutherford B. Hayes after making a call from
Washington to Pennsylvania with Alexander
Graham Bell's telephone

I have what I believe are some good ideas for a few inventions. I realize I should probably go ahead and make a prototype and patent these myself, but I'm too busy. Or too giving. Okay, too lazy. If anyone out there wants to work on them though, I'd be happy to talk to you about sharing a portion of the profits. The fact is, I just want to see these inventions on the market.

Have you ever felt that way about an idea? You know it could make you wealthy, but *Jeopardy* is on and you just don't have the time or the energy to do the legwork for your million-dollar idea. Besides, what if it did earn you a million dollars? There would be all those bank deposits that you'd have to make, employees you'd have to hire, and you'd need a warehouse to store your product (your coffee table can only hold so much). If you ask me, it all sounds like one big headache. When you figure all the time it's going to consume of your life, sometimes what you'd really rather do is just go to the store, buy the product, and be done with it. Let someone else do the production and marketing work. Let someone else keep track of the sales. Let someone else make the infomercial and hype the audience into their "Oooohs" and "Ahhhhs." Let someone else deal with all the paper work and the wheeling and dealing. You just want to be able to go to Wal-Mart and buy the product.

That's how I feel about these ideas.

The first thing I wish someone would invent is a Husband Leash. Never mind those kiddie leashes. Most mothers and grandmothers have no problem keeping track of their offspring. What women really need is a leash for their husbands, especially in the mall. In fact, maybe malls could let you check them out like they do the kiddie strollers. When a husband leaves his wife in the sportswear department and goes to find a chair, he can easily end up two stores away without a clue in the world of where he is. Even broadcasting his name over the PA doesn't help because he may not be within earshot of the announcement. Some husbands have probably been divorced on the grounds of desertion, when all they did was wander into the wrong store at the mall.

I also think someone should invent a Cell Phone Disintegrator. This would work a lot like those laser guns that police use on speeders, except the Cell Phone Disintegrator would actually shoot a laser to the cell phone and instantly disintegrate it in the caller's hand, without harm or injury to the caller. Imagine the fun we'd have aiming it at those rudest of cell phone users that we encounter throughout our day, and watching the look on their faces as their phone mysteriously disintegrates right in their hands. You could use it in restaurants, in movie theaters, in elevators, in department stores; anywhere and everywhere you encounter people talking incessantly on their cell phone with no regard for those around them.

Another idea I would like to see invented is the Back of the Throat Scratcher. You know that scratchy feeling you can get in the back of your throat, especially during allergy season? The one that drives you to make that irritating noise with your throat, trying to make the vibrations "scratch" the area for you, but it only temporarily solves the problem? That's where the Back of the Throat Scratcher would come in. It would work like a back scratcher, only instead of scratching your back, you would be using it on your throat. The biggest problem I can see encountering with this invention is the gag reflex, but I'm sure that can be worked out.

And you know how car manufacturers now offer heated seats to warm you on those chilly mornings? Why can't that same technology give us heated clothes? Sure, we might have to stay near an outlet to plug in our pants or shirt, but the concept does have merit, don't you think? It'd be a tough sell to menopausal women, because of the heat issue, but men (especially the ones who tend to turn up the thermostat in their homes fourteen seconds after their hot-flashing wives have turned it down) would probably love it.

I also think someone should improve on the car wash. If we're going to be sitting in our car and going through the process anyway, why not make it a little more entertaining? Synchronize the giant brushes to '50s songs, add some laser lights, and make it a whole multi-media experience.

I can't help it, these million-dollar ideas just come to me.

I think the older we get, the more ideas like this pop into our heads. My father used to sit and draw out elaborate plans for all sorts of inventions, often on a dinner napkin. Some of the ideas and plans were pretty amazing. Maybe even brilliant. Unfortunately, he never did anything with those ideas. He passed away before trying to create it or applying for a patent. He never got past the napkin stage.

Who knows what kind of million-dollar ideas are floating around in your head, too. If you think you've got a good idea in you, do something with it. Who knows? Maybe your idea will be the next major discovery. Maybe it'll change life as we know it today.

Or maybe it'll just be another way to get rid of that throat itch. Whatever it is, don't let it just sit there on your napkin. Napkins are for wiping up messes. Not for genius.

The true creator is necessity, who is the mother of our invention.
—Plato

Dreaming Your Life Away

*Never laugh at anyone's dreams. People who
don't have dreams don't have much.*
—Unknown

One of my father's favorite things to do was to browse
through farm real estate catalogs and circle the ads of whatever properties happened to catch his eye. Some would be
spreads of twenty acres, some fifty, and a few would be a
hundred or more. It didn't matter how large or how small the
farm was, my dad would dream about buying it and living
there one day. Dad had grown up on a farm and spent a lot of
time thinking about returning to his roots someday.

Unfortunately, he passed away before ever making that
move and seeing his dream fulfilled. The closest he got to
returning to farm life was those catalogs and his dreams.

My mother had dreams, too. One of those dreams was to
see Washington, D.C. After my father passed away, leaving

more circled ads in farmland magazines than footprints in green pastures, I determined that the same thing wasn't going to happen to at least one of my mother's dreams. So early one morning I "kidnapped" her and we flew to our nation's capital. It took some secretive planning on my part. I had to call her work and prearrange for her to have the time off. Then I needed to make the flight and hotel reservations and plan out our itinerary. It took a little extra effort, but looking back on it now, I am so glad that I did what I could to help fulfill this one particular dream of my mother's. Especially since a few years after that trip, she developed lymphoma, and due to her frequent chemotherapy treatments, travel was all too quickly out of the question.

Lesson learned? Life is too short not to fulfill or at least attempt to fulfill our dreams and the dreams of our loved ones. As long as our dreams are healthy, legal, and don't hurt anyone else, we should do everything we can to go after them. Too many people get to the end of their lives realizing that they did nothing except ponder the great "what might have beens" of their life.

Have you thought much about what dreams you might be postponing? What are you circling in catalogs and brochures and travel books? Where have you always wanted to visit or perhaps even move to? What have you dreamed of accomplishing? Or maybe just attempting? What talent lies within you that has yet to be released? What is your passion? What were you created to do that, for whatever reason, you have been postponing year after year after year? What is your dream and, more importantly, why are you waiting to do anything about fulfilling it?

Start putting your talents to work today, not tomorrow. Give your passion the attention it deserves. Whether it be teaching, singing, building, learning, traveling, or whatever else you've been longing to do, give yourself permission to do it. Your dream has waited long enough.

It's important to remember, though, that all you have power over is the pursuit of your dream, the attempt, and the perseverance. The outcome is not in your hands. Still, it's not the outcome that brings you all the satisfaction. There is a good feeling that comes from merely having attempted to follow your dreams. Succeed or fail, at least you know you tried.

Not one of us is going to get to the end of our lives and be handed a refund for our unfulfilled dreams and plans.

"Oh, I'm sorry. I see here on your life report that you never did fulfill that dream of becoming a professional baseball player. Okay, here's your youth back. Go give it another shot."

Life doesn't happen that way. If we want to fulfill our dreams, timing is everything. And there will be for all of us dreams that we can't go back and force to come true. We just have to accept that. It would be difficult for a sixty-five-year-old woman, no matter how attractive she may be, to fulfill her dream of becoming Miss America. By the same token, a fifty-five-year-old, 118-pound man will probably never fulfill his dream of becoming a professional football player, even if he can play a pretty good game with his grandchildren. Fifty-five-year-old bones are still fifty-five-year-old bones.

But the dreams that are still within our grasp, the ones that carry a degree of possibility, the ones that still burn inside us, those are the ones that we shouldn't give up on.

It comes down to this: While we're waiting for the "right" time, the *only* time we have is passing us by. While we're waiting for "perfect" circumstances, the *only* circumstances we're ever going to be offered are leaving us behind. We can plan all we want, dream all we want, hope all we want, but eventually it's up to us to take that first step. There is nothing sadder than someone reaching the final chapter of their life and having nothing to look back on except regrets.

So don't forget, there is more than one way of fulfilling your dreams. If you've always dreamed of becoming a doctor, but circumstances, responsibilities, and maybe your grade-point average has kept you from pursuing that career, you can still apply for a job or volunteer for a position in the medical industry. If you've always dreamed of traveling the world but don't have the funds to do it, maybe you could look into getting a part-time job at a travel agency. There are plenty of travel perks for people in the travel business. Who knows—you just might be able to earn money and see the world, too. Whatever it is you want to do, if you put your mind to it, you can probably find a way to either fulfill your dream or at least get a taste of it.

So go after your dreams. Celebrate the portion of your life that lies ahead of you, and don't fall into the trap of thinking it's too late. We may not have our yesterdays, but we have today and tomorrow. Don't waste them.

Whatever you can do, or dream you can, begin it. Boldness has genius, power, and magic in it. Begin it now.

—Goethe

Mind Games

Exercise is a dirty word. Every time I hear it,
I wash my mouth out with chocolate.
—Author Unknown

Have you ever watched another person do something physically straining, only to get worn out yourself? You haven't moved a muscle (unless you count eye muscles), but you're exhausted just from watching someone else get a workout.

Last Christmas I went with my daughter-in-law and granddaughter to a local ballet company's performance of *The Nutcracker Suite,* and I came home so weak I could barely put one foot in front of the other. For the duration of the ballet, I had been right there on stage with all the other dancers, doing every move they did. At least in my head. I was balancing myself on my toes, doing pirouettes, jumps, and leg lifts. By the next morning I was so sore I couldn't even get out of bed! My brain ballet had drained every ounce of energy out of me. I had leg cramps, and I think I even pulled a groin muscle. It's a good thing we didn't go see *Riverdance*; I could have ended up in traction.

This sort of thing always happens to me when I watch someone else do physically demanding activities. If I'm watching the World Series on television, I'll picture myself out there in the batter's box hitting a home run and running around the bases. I'm huffing and puffing so much by the second inning that I've got to take a nap.

If I watch basketball, in my mind I'm out there on the court, running with the team, making basket after basket, dribbling, shooting, guarding. I usually hold up pretty well until we get into the second minute of the game, and by then I'm so winded I have to imagine myself sitting on the bench for a while just so I can catch my breath.

If my neighbors are jogging down our street, I'll picture myself running alongside them (okay, a few blocks behind them), but I'm out there just the same. Then I imagine shin splints and have to stop.

I've had to give up watching the Olympics altogether. I almost blew a lung in the weightlifting competition. Luckily I turned the channel before I killed myself.

The problem is this—in my mind I have the ability to dance on my toes, jump rope for hours, lift weights, and run a four-hour marathon. No matter what I imagine myself doing, the realist in me fast-forwards to the end result, and that usually involves injury or extreme exhaustion. On one level I suppose it's a good quality. It keeps me from actually doing certain activities where I could get injured in real life. But on the other hand, it's taking all the enjoyment out of watching organized sports, ballet, or other physically demanding activities and competitions.

Long ago I accepted the fact that my face will never be on the cover of a box of Wheaties. Shredded Wheat, maybe, but Wheaties, no. I'm not the kind of person who inspires people to physical excellence. My motto isn't Feel the Burn, it's Feel the Bed. Last month I thought I'd found the perfect gym for me and bought a one-year membership, but the staff at Gymboree keep making me get off the plastic castle and let the kids have a turn.

Still, they tell us that at our age it's important to keep moving, to treat our bodies as a musical instrument and always keep it tuned. But I've seen myself from behind—I'm a set of bagpipes when I'd rather be a violin.

But facts don't lie, and the facts show that the more exercising we do, the healthier we're going to be. The problem I have, though, is figuring out what's the best exercise for me.

I've tried exercise equipment. My son bought his wife the Gazelle for her birthday, and she's been letting me use it. I really like it. It's a little like skiing, only without the frostbite. Once you learn how to balance yourself on it, it's a lot of fun.

I've also tried walking, biking, bowling, aerobics, Pilates, and just about everything else you can think of.

But I may have finally found the ideal exercise program for me. According to a new study by the Mayo Clinic, even those of us who live a sedentary lifestyle can burn around 350 calories a day from just all those routine movements we do every day, including fidgeting. That's right, fidgeting. So that's the exercise program I'm on now. The Fidget Plan. It's perfect for me. I might not be able to complete a single push-up, but I can fidget for hours. I could become a triathlon athlete in this competition. I can do all sorts of fidgeting. I can tap my fingers on the table, cross my legs, and swing my top leg back and forth faster and longer than most. I am a champion fidgeter.

But why not go for the gold? Why don't I increase all my nervous habits and movements and let them burn off even more calories and get me in shape? Eye twitches, fingernail biting, scratching, yawning, I can do it all!

But later. Right now I'm watching Wimbledon and I'm exhausted!

The human body was designed to walk, run or stop; it wasn't built for coasting.
—Cullen Hightower

Alma Maters Matter

The secret of life is honesty and fair dealing.
If you can fake that, you've got it made.
—Groucho Marx

I just read an article about an Internet "school" based in Texas that rewarded a college degree to a cat. The scam might have continued to go unnoticed, but apparently the cat was throwing fraternity parties and hanging out until all hours of the night.

All right, the cat only threw *one* fraternity party. But I'm serious about the degree. This six-year-old cat really did receive an MBA from an Internet "university" in Texas. As gifted as the cat might very well have been, the school, according to the article and lawsuit, didn't even offer classes. It was allegedly just a front for fake degrees. Poor cat. Now that the scam has been uncovered, he'll probably lose his accounting job.

It does bring up a good point, though. Scams are everywhere. And apparently, plenty of them are on the Internet. You can get just about anything you want in cyberspace these days. Want a Bachelor of Arts degree? Pay the money and print up a form. A doctorate? Pay the money and print up a form. Want to be valedictorian of your class, graduate with honors, be named "Most Likely to Succeed"? Pay a little extra and print up a form. If you've got the ink, apparently you can have the "degree," "certificate," or whatever else you happen to desire.

It doesn't only happen there, though. A writer friend of mine once filled out a biographical form for one of those generic *Who's Who* books. For laughs, he listed all sorts of outrageous credits, including serving a term as vice-president of the United States. Amazingly enough, they printed it! Now granted, many of *us* probably wouldn't be able to name all the vice-presidents from the past several decades, but you would think that a company would be required to do a little bit of research before they print whatever someone sends them. But since this probably wasn't a legitimate *Who's Who* book, no research was done. The book was printed, listing whatever credits he had sent them. For him it was just a prank to see if they really would print it, and he got a good laugh out of it all. For them, however, it seemed to be more of "if the check clears, you can have the credit."

Now, for the record, I'm listed in several *Who's Who* books myself. Well, actually my listings are just in a *Who?* book.

If getting all these "credits" is this easy, though, it does make you wonder about the "professional" people in your life, doesn't it? For instance, is that diploma that's hanging on the wall of your dentist's office one that he actually earned from an accredited dental school, or will your root canal involve garden tools? Is that plumber you found in the phone book someone with legitimate trade school training and twenty years of experience like his ad says, or will you have the next Old Faithful erupting in your living room? And what about the pilot on the airplane you're flying in? Did he get his license off the *i.r.a.pilot.com* Web site?

When did we get so gullible? Why don't we question more? If the doctor we go to has a degree from Phil's Medical Night School and Garage, maybe we should find someone else. If someone tries to tell us how to invest our money and they're driving a rusted '69 Volkswagen bus, maybe we ought to double-check their financial advice. If we meet someone who shares an unbelievable story of hardship, then asks us for a donation, maybe "unbelievable" should be the key word. It's up to us to check out their story before we write the check. Some people will do or say anything for attention or money. Middle-agers and seniors have been the target of scams for years, and the only way to stop it is to become more aware.

We shouldn't allow ourselves to get talked into car repairs we don't need, roofing projects that could have waited, a new vacuum cleaner when we have a perfectly good one that works, encyclopedias that we probably will never open, candy and cookies that cost twice the price of what you could get them for at a store, driveway cleaner that we use the first day and then put it away never to look at again, drums of laundry detergent too big to store in our laundry room, parcels of land we haven't even seen, gold mines and oil wells that probably dried up years ago. In so many situations we stand to lose a lot of our hard-earned money, or in some cases it could be our health, all because we didn't take the time to check things out for ourselves. Or we simply had trouble saying that one simple two-letter word: no.

If we don't do our part to help get a handle on these types of situations, who knows how bad things could get. I mean, if a cat can get an MBA, other animals might start trying to get degrees, too. Instead of being your best friend, your dog could soon be your boss. One day he could take you aside (after a course in English as a Second Language), and say,

"Sorry, pops, but I'm going to have to let you go."

"Let me go? But why? I thought you were my best friend."

"You've been late for walking me four nights in a row now. We haven't played Frisbee in over a month. And food from a can? Puh-leeeeeease. All this is completely unacceptable. Now pack your things and be out of the house by noon! I'll be interviewing replacement owners first thing tomorrow morning. And get out of that recliner. That's my seat now. You're shedding your hair all over it."

"I am not shedding hair."

"Hey, I'm just calling it like I see it. You're the one with the bald spot, not me!"

But before you move out, call the university and check out the legitimacy of his degree. If it's from a fraudulent Internet university, you can keep your seat. But now, if you find it's from a legitimate Internet school, well, your only recourse is to make him pay back his own student loans.

> **It is better to deserve an honor and not receive it, than to receive one, and not deserve it!**
> —Mark Twain

28

Of All Places

**_Always have your bags packed; you never know
where life's journey is going to take you._**
—Appalachian saying

By the time you reach middle age, chances are you've done a
lot of housework. And that housework has no doubt included
cleaning that one item we all hate to clean—the toilet bowl.
But we do it because we realize that if we want to live in sani-
tary conditions, that's one chore that has to be done.

In the house where I grew up, my mother was usually the
one who cleaned the toilet. Every once in a while, though,
one of us kids would do it. It wasn't as much fun as playing a
game of Monopoly or Old Maid, but we did it and survived.

In the four houses that my husband and I have lived in
during our marriage, we've shared the toilet cleaning duties
in each one. I have also cleaned toilets in other people's
homes and at various churches, as the need arose. I've
cleaned all kinds of bowls—new ones, rusted ones, broken
ones, old-fashioned ones, elongated ones, and water-saving
ones. In all my years of cleaning toilets, however, nothing like

the story that I'm about to tell you has ever happened to me!

Apparently, a few years ago a woman in Longview, Texas, came home to find that her toilet was bubbling up oil. That's right—she struck *oil* right there in her toilet. This Longview, Texas, woman hit a gusher in her flusher!

Now, before you scoff, you should know that this wasn't an article that I read in some supermarket tabloid, nor is it one of those hoaxes that continually circle the Internet until we've all passed it around 487 times and have fallen for it 487 times. No, CNN, MSNBC, and the Associated Press all reported this story. It's true, down to the very last gooey drop of black Texas gold. The woman's years of cleaning toilets finally paid off for her. Instead of calling a plumber, the woman could call her accountant and tell him that she had finally found her pot of gold at the end of the rainbow, or in this case, at the end of the pot.

But why did this happen in the first place? And why don't more of us get a tip like this for our housecleaning services? All I've ever gotten for cleaning the bathroom is a backache.

Well, one theory is that the woman's house might have been built on top of an old abandoned well that wasn't adequately capped and suddenly started gushing oil out of whatever pipeline it could find. Whatever the reason, the bottom line is that the lady struck oil in the last place on earth anyone would be looking for it. Let's face it, when's the last time anyone ever listed their toilet as an asset on their balance sheet?

This discovery has to have a positive effect on families all across Texas, and perhaps even the world, though. Families will no longer fight over *not* doing the household chores.

"*Hey, it's my turn to clean the toilet!*"

"*No way! You got to clean it last time!*"

"*Mommmmmyyyyy! Rickey won't let me clean the toilet!*"

And now that I think about it, who knows how many other household chores might someday reap a similar benefit? Maybe there's a diamond mine in the midst of all those dust bunnies under our beds. Or gold nuggets just waiting to be panned in our dishwater. There might even be an abandoned silver mine in the back of our closet. Who knows what fortunes are waiting to be discovered with a little elbow grease? At long last our housecleaning duties just might be finally set to pay off!

> **Content makes poor men rich; discontentment makes rich men poor.**
> —Benjamin Franklin

Social Security

Parody of "Falling in Love Again," sung in the style of Marlene Dietrich:

> Social Security,
> paid our whole lives through,
> now that it's come due,
> *where is it?!*

30

What's in Your Pocket?

My doctor gave me six months to live, but when I couldn't pay the bill he gave me six months more.
—Walter Matthau

Perhaps you've seen it—the at-home defibrillator. They've been advertising it everywhere, and personally I think the idea is long overdue. There is no telling how many lives a product like this is going to save. Imagine not having to wait for emergency medical care to arrive. Now a defibrillator can be as close as your pocket.

As amazing as this new product is, though, it makes you wonder what other "pocket" medical equipment could follow, especially if the ever-expanding infomercial market starts getting in on the action and comes up with a few of these inventions. We might soon be seeing products like:

The Gall Bladder Eggstractor

The Arterial Blockage Blaster
The Post-Surgical Stitch and Buttoneer
Liver Spot Instagone
Pop-a-Dent Cellulite Removal Kit
Ginsu Face-Lift Surgical Knife Set
The Internal Organ Pocket Navigator (for all your at-home surgical needs)

And that's just the beginning. Whether we'll ever see any products like the above (probably not) or whether researchers are already working on something a whole lot better, one thing is for sure—incredible advances are being made in the field of home medical testing and monitoring. Millions of people living with chronic diseases such as diabetes, heart disease, high blood pressure, and more are all benefiting from these medical and technological breakthroughs.

But now if they ever do come out with Liver Spot Instagone, I'm ordering a five-gallon can and a paint roller.

Our doctor would never really operate unless it was necessary. He was just that way. If he didn't need the money, he wouldn't lay a hand on you.
—Herb Shriner

31

Tattoo to You, Too

**You don't stop laughing because you grow old;
you grow old because you stop laughing.**
—Michael Pritchard

I'm thinking about getting a tattoo. Now before you get the impression that I'm some kind of middle-aged rebel, let me explain. It's not really a tattoo, at least not in the anchor, Harley, or "Mom" kind of way. It's not even a rose or a butterfly. The tattoo I'm wanting is, well, it's an eyebrow. No, not an extra one; I'm not looking to start a new trend or anything like that. It's just that I've been a half-eyebrow short for some time now and I would very much like to have the missing half permanently drawn back on. From what I understand, they can do this now by sort of tattooing on permanent makeup. An interesting, albeit not totally painless, idea. The pain part isn't something I would look forward to, but I would certainly welcome the opportunity to at long last wake up in the morning and not look like a descendent of Spock from *Star Trek*.

I don't know why fifty percent of my left eyebrow decided

to go AWOL in the first place. All I know is that some years ago, half of my left eyebrow took off to places unknown, and to this day it hasn't returned to camp. I've been having to fill it in with an eyebrow pencil, but the problem is some days I forget.

I remember this same thing happening to my father. His eyebrow suddenly stopped growing, too, so maybe it's hereditary. We've never been tested, but perhaps my family lacks the eyebrow gene. Or maybe we have a weak one floating around in our DNA. I suppose my own offspring could get their DNA genetically altered so that future descendents can have the eyebrows that God originally intended, but that could be expensive.

But I am a little apprehensive. Every once in a while the news will report a story of someone who tried to improve their looks by some procedure and never made it out of the clinic alive. Something went horribly wrong, and what should have been relatively minor and routine, turned deadly. Would I really want my cause of death to be listed as an eyebrow tattoo? Would my insurance policy even pay out on that? And what about my funeral? I could just imagine the comments.

"Why couldn't she have lived with it? It was just a lousy eyebrow, for crying out loud."

"I know, but she must have gone peacefully. Just look at how relaxed her good brow looks."

When you think about it, what do we really need our eyebrows for anyway? They don't provide a life-sustaining function or anything like that. They don't shade us from the sun. Most of the time our eyebrows just sit there on top of our eyes trying to stay out of the way of all the other facial parts. They're relatively passive. How else can they be? We make sure they don't dare grow beyond their borders. If they do, we women immediately get out the tweezers and start plucking them back into submission.

But since eyebrows do help balance out our faces, I'm looking into my options. It's either a tattoo or shave the other eyebrow to match.

Nobody really cares if you're miserable, so you might as well be happy.
—Cynthia Nelms

It's All Downhill From Here

There is no thrill quite like doing something you didn't know you could.
—Marjorie Holmes

I did it. I never really wanted to do it, never thought I could do it, didn't even dream about doing it, but I did it. It's amazing the things you can talk yourself into doing when you're on a ladies' retreat with some forty-five other women in the mountains of Montana. You begin to feel courageous, daring, and maybe even a little bit coordinated. (Okay, maybe not coordinated. But definitely daring and courageous.)

Before that day the thought of going down the side of a mountain on a pair of skis had never even once appealed to me. Mainly because I instinctively knew I wouldn't look good in a body cast. (Body casts can make you look two sizes heavier.)

But then I saw the other ladies donning their snowsuits

and getting fitted for ski equipment, and something inside of me rose up and said, *"I shall not let the fear of landing upside down in the snow stand in my way! I shall not be a wimp! I shall prove to myself that I can do whatever I set my mind to do!"* (I didn't know what it was that rose up inside of me, but it sure was wordy.)

Before I knew it, me and my courage were in the rental shop trying on a pair of skis and filling out a form for whom to notify in case I died in some sort of freak ski entanglement accident on the bunny slope.

I didn't know the first thing about skiing, but our hostess, Kay Creech, had graciously offered a ski lesson to anyone who wanted one. Comforted by the support of about forty other women, I decided to take Kay up on the offer. When else would I ever sign up for a ski lesson?

So I dialed my husband on my cell phone. "I think I'll go skiing this afternoon, honey, maybe take a lesson," I said.

"You? On a pair of skis? Have you forgotten about *Les Misérables*?"

Les Misérables is our code word for, well, *Les Misérables,* and it's enough to snap me out of any physical activity requiring coordination. *Les Misérables* was another downhill experience, only without the skis, and it happened when my daughter-in-law and I were in New York to see the Broadway musical. During intermission, I walked upstairs to use the rest room. When they flashed the lights indicating that intermission was now over, I attempted to rush back to my seat, but my foot slipped as I began down the stairs, and my descent then picked up quite a bit of speed as I tumbled head over feet all the way down. And I was wearing a skirt. My body came to rest at the bottom of the stairs, at the foot of a security guard and dozens of onlookers. I was in pain, but thanks to the good time I had made due to the fall, I wasn't late for the next act.

But with friends like Sue Buchanan, Julie Barnhill, Kay Creech, Cindy Creech, and so many others encouraging me to give it a try, I got the courage to do it. After all, what hot-flashing middle-aged woman wouldn't want to spend an afternoon sliding around in snow and icy slush?

Our ski instructor, Link Neimark, is one of the top in the field. He's a PSIA Level III, a USSA Alpine Race Coach, and has over twenty-five years' experience. Or to put it another way, in the photos of our first lessons, he was always the one standing upright.

At first, the only coordination I had out there on the snow was my outfit. I had borrowed a black snowsuit from one of the ladies, and wore a black fleece jacket over it. (I figured black would be a suitable color. In case anything should go wrong, I would already be dressed for the funeral.) I also wore a tan jacket over the black one because they say when you're going to be out in the winter elements, it's best to layer your clothing. I was so layered, I was like a torte on skis.

And then there was the pink hat. All of the ladies in our group wore pink hats that we had decorated the night before with various pieces of costume jewelry and rhinestones and such. Gluing and stitching seemed like too much work, so all I did to decorate mine was write on it with a black Sharpie the words, "If found upside down with skis pointing heavenward, please call . . ." and I listed my phone number.

Link was very helpful and encouraging to each of us in the beginning group. He let us go at our own pace. It didn't take long for the other two gals in my group to advance and move on to bigger and better runs. I was a little more cautious. I knew that even though my pink hat did have my phone number listed on it, being buried in the snow would not be a good thing.

After a while I managed to actually take a few steps in the skis. Then I fell. I tried to get up, but my feet were stuck in one position, with my legs wanting to go in another. No matter how hard I tried, they refused to work together.

I finally did manage to get back up, and as it turned out, that was the only time I fell that day. Thanks to our encouraging instructor who never once laughed at me, and the fact that I was among friends and wanting to see my husband's face when he looked at the pictures of me "skiing," I hung in there and I can now say that I have skied.

Okay, the bunny slope.

Okay, the bottom third of the bunny slope.

I can also say that I learned a lot about myself that day. I learned that if I want to do something, I can achieve it at least on some level. I know that I'll never be an Olympic skier. I might not even ever ski again. But I did do it once, and I'm pretty proud of myself for that. I didn't break a single bone. By comparison, I once broke a toe just stepping up onto my front porch.

So maybe the motivational people are right. Maybe we shouldn't let our fears control our lives. Maybe life is really just a string of situations where we've faced our fears and learned that we could indeed do whatever it was we were afraid of.

Fear is a party pooper. What have you been letting it keep you from doing? Be courageous; who knows what exhilarating new experiences are awaiting you.

You must do the thing you think you cannot do.
—Eleanor Roosevelt

That Settles It

Avoid any diet which discourages the use of hot fudge.
—Don Kardong

I would like to know why I was awarded a little pouch in my midsection the minute I hit middle age. It's like I'm wearing a fanny pack around my waist. Only I'm not. It's all me. I am the fanny pack. Like my under-the-chin skin, this situation also appeared without warning, without permission, and definitely without a welcome. Overnight I went from being able to fit perfectly into my jeans to not even being able to fasten them. The button and buttonhole are farther apart than the Republicans and Democrats. No matter how hard I try to push the two sides together, I can't seem to get them to meet. There is just way too much of me in the way.

Some have referred to this as the middle-age spread, which makes sense, I suppose. After all, it's probably the result of a lot of spreads—butter, cream cheese, whipped topping, cake frosting . . .

I can recall a time when I never used to have to think

about my stomach. My father was tall and lean in his younger days, and I guess I had taken after him. My stomach has been perfectly flat for most of my life.

But now the pouch has arrived. I've tried to suck it in, but it won't budge. Apparently it likes it just fine where it's at.

It's a lot more prominent when I sit. Sometimes I feel like I'm holding a globe in my lap. It's round and protruding and whenever I look down at it, I can't help but wonder if I might be able to balance my coffee on it.

I guess the best way to describe what has happened to me is that I've "settled." You know how a house settles? Sometimes the repairs are merely cosmetic. Other times you need to call in the plumbers and hard-hat workers. Well, that's what it feels like my body has done. Some of the settling has required minor repairs. The rest has needed plumbers and hard-hat workers.

My body has even started making those settling noises, especially in the joints. You know that creaking sound that reminds you of a loose gate on an abandoned farm? My knees sound like that every time I get up from the sofa.

But even with all the settling, the creaking, the middle-age spreading, and the skin loosening, one thing's for certain: there is plenty to laugh about in the second half of our lives. And as long as our foundations don't crack, we're home free.

Old age is no place for sissies.
—Bette Davis

Relaxation Island

There cannot be a crisis next week.
My schedule is already full.
—Dr. Henry Kissinger

Some of the hottest merchandise on the market today is relaxation products. You can buy waterfall machines, neck massagers, back massagers, and sound therapy CDs that will play the sounds of a babbling brook, ocean waves, birds chirping, and just about any other relaxing sounds you can think of. (Funny, you never see a relaxation tape called "nagging wife" or "belching husband." But I digress.)

These products are great, and in our highly stressful world, probably very much needed.

But have you ever wondered how differently we would conduct our lives if we all had blood pressure and stress monitors hooked up to us twenty-four hours a day? If we knew the effect that high-stress situations had on our health, would we continue trying to right every wrong that is dealt us, or would we learn how to let a few of them slide? I have a feeling we'd start letting a *lot* of things slide.

Sure, it feels good to be right. But it also feels good to just *be*—as in being alive. Some disagreements and pettiness just aren't worth our getting involved in.

I wonder, too, how watching news programs affects our blood pressure and health. Every time the Homeland Security Alert rises to a new level, surely our stress indicators have to be rising right along with it. We can try to brush it off and go about our day, but it's not always easy to shake that feeling of impending doom. The "What if" scenarios are endless. What if there's anthrax on my mail? What if gas prices top three dollars a gallon? What if the terrorists attack Wal-Mart? There is so much more to worry about these days, it's a wonder we're not all hiding under our beds. What if. . . ? What if. . . ? What if. . . ? We can "What if?" ourselves right into a heart attack if we're not careful.

And what are all the political debates and commentaries doing to us? Tossing pillows at some politician or news anchor's image on the television screen might make us feel better for the moment, but it won't keep our blood pressure from rising over the long haul. Of course, even though we have the ability to turn off these news programs with the click of a remote control, many of us will stay glued to the television screen on a big news day, watching the same news story rerun itself into the wee hours of the morning, over and over and over again.

Maybe it would benefit us all if we would just go on a news-free diet, if even for a few days, just to see how much better we'd feel. This is a popular recommendation for people under stress, and I think it's a great idea. You don't even have to check with your doctor to begin this kind of health plan. Just turn off the news for one week and see how much brighter your outlook becomes and how much more relaxed you feel.

Another way to relax is to take a nice hot bath. There are all sorts of homemade soaps and bath additives that can turn your regular bathtub into a spa of sorts. You might also think about turning on some soft music and surrounding the bathtub with burning candles. Not only will this relax you, but if your hair happens to catch on fire from the candles, you've got plenty of water right there to put it out.

Aquariums are supposed to help lower our blood pressure and relax us, too. There's something soothing about watching fish with nothing better to do than swim around all day. They have it made. They're fed when they're hungry, and someone else even cleans their tank for them.

But we could learn a lot from aquarium fish. They know how to entertain themselves. You don't see them sitting in a corner looking bored with their life. All they do all day is swim around in circles, but they know how to make it interesting. They take a different path every time they go around the tank. It may be the same tank day in and day out, but they find creative ways to make the same-old same-old a little more interesting. Sometimes they'll dive to the bottom of the tank. Other times they'll swim up to the top. They'll go in and out of the underwater castle or the ceramic sunken ship.

They'll swim over to the light and check that out for a while. They might turn around and swim a different direction, then suddenly turn around again just for fun. They know how to make their restricted lives spontaneous and fun.

But how many of us humans are in a rut, doing the same old thing every day, with boredom written all over our faces? We drive the same road to the bank, walk the same path every night, go to the same grocery store, the same mall, the same gas station, and we're Bored with a capital B.

Perhaps we should try to be more like aquarium fish. Maybe we could start taking a different road into town. We could try out a new recipe, walk in a different park, go to a different grocery store, do something out of the ordinary. Who knows? We just might like it. At the very least, it will break up our monotony.

Another thing we can do is travel. If we have the health and the funds, we should start seeing those parts of the world that we've always wanted to see. If we have no one else to go with, we could go with a tour group. You know what they say—change your scenery and you'll change your outlook.

But whatever we do, however we relax, the important thing to remember is to keep our daily stresses down to a minimum. Deal with those situations that need to be dealt with, and leave alone the ones that are just time and energy drainers. We'll be a whole lot healthier for it.

I could go on and on about how to not let stress get the best of us, but the presidential debates just aired and now all the political pundits are putting in their two cents' worth. In other words, it's time to start tossing pillows at the television set again.

> ***Worrying is like a rocking chair: it gives you
> something to do, but it doesn't get
> you anywhere.***
> —Anonymous

Tuesdays With Metamucil

I am a nutritional overachiever.
—Author Unknown

Have you ever wondered why it is that the older we get, the more preoccupied we become with our digestive and intestinal tracks? Take for instance roughage. Why do people our age obsess over roughage? I don't remember doing that when I was younger. I don't remember ever once asking my mother if she packed a bran muffin in my lunch pail because I wasn't really "feeling like myself" that day.

Frankly, I don't know anyone who truly likes bran. If bran were a popular flavor, we'd see bran-flavored chewing gum, bran-flavored Sno-Kones, Bran Coke and Bran Pepsi, and bran would be the thirty-second flavor of ice cream at Baskin-Robbins.

But bran isn't a popular flavor. Most of us wouldn't eat it if it wasn't for the health benefits of it. If the government were to issue a warning tomorrow admitting that they were wrong and bran in fact causes many health ailments and should not be eaten, we'd be tossing out our muffins so fast the sanitation workers couldn't keep up with it. (Or lift the bags either.)

That's never going to happen, though, because apparently bran is good for us.

I think I liked it better before all of this health consciousness. We could order the foods we liked, foods with high fat and low fiber content, foods with (I know I'm being politically incorrect here, but I have to be honest) *carbs*, and we didn't have a single ounce of guilt over any of it.

But then along came the carb counting, the good and bad cholesterol monitoring, and twenty-eight-grain breads, and all the fun shot right out of our whole dining experience. (By the way, just out of curiosity, exactly how many grains does a loaf of bread require before it is reclassified as lumber and sold at The Home Depot instead?)

Roughage isn't the only thing that we become obsessed with as we get older. We start paying closer attention to how much fat, sugar, sodium, carbs, cholesterol, and chili pepper we're putting into our mouths, too. We read the nutritional labels on packages like they're Grisham novels, and we carry bottles of drinking water around throughout our day to make sure we're getting all the fluids we need.

We try to stay up-to-date on all the latest nutritional discoveries, too. If we read an article about some new food item or vitamin or mineral supplement that's supposed to be healthy for us, we're at the grocery store buying a crate of it that same day.

Ever since I learned how healthy salmon is for us, I've been ordering it almost every time I go out to dinner. I don't even like salmon; I just eat it because I know it's good for me. Now I find out that there's a difference between farm-raised salmon and fished salmon, so I don't know if I've been helping myself or hurting myself. Who knows? I only know that I'm not going to be a happy camper if I've been opting for salmon when I could have been eating a cheeseburger and fries all this time.

If they do ever switch on us and confess that they were wrong about everything, wrong about carbs (we can have all we want), wrong about sugar (the more the merrier), wrong about fat (go ahead, indulge!), wrong about sodium, cholesterol, chili pepper, and all the rest, there's going to be a revolt in this country the likes of which we've never seen before. Riots will break out in front of health food stores! People will be having bran bonfires, and considering the woody texture, the fire might burn for years. Posters of famous nutritionists and diet book writers, with a giant circle drawn around their faces with a line through it, will be carried through the streets! Exercise equipment will be thrown through the glass doors at gym and health clubs! Unless cooler heads prevail, it is not going to be pretty, people.

Husband to his wife: "You could lose a lot of weight if you'd just carry all your diet books around the block once a day."
—Bill Hoest (*The Lockhorns*)

Thanks, But No Thanks

Gratitude is not only the greatest of virtues,
but the parent of all others.
—Cicero

Not long ago, Oprah Winfrey and Pontiac gave away G6 sedans to Oprah's entire studio audience, consisting of 276 people. Apparently, this incredible display of generosity rang in at a price of around seven million dollars. When presented with their gift, tears of joy overwhelmed the recipients. That is, until they discovered they would need to pay the taxes on the cars out of their own pockets. It was then that a few of the recipients seemed to change their attitude and decided to bite or at least nibble on the hand that extended the car keys.

Now granted, paying the taxes on a brand-new car would certainly be a problem for someone who couldn't afford to buy the car in the first place. So on one level the complaints might be a little understandable. But weren't there other ways to remedy the situation other than complaining to the news media? Selling the car, taking the equally needed cash, and buying a less expensive used car might have been one choice. As far as I know, no one was forcing anyone to keep their brand-new cars. I may be wrong, but I'm pretty sure it was their option to either accept the gift, give it back, or trade it in for something else, just like any of us could do with any of the gifts we receive. If your Aunt Agnes gives you a pair of armadillo bedroom slippers next Christmas, you would probably exercise your right to take the slippers back to the store and use the cash or store credit for whatever else you might want (if your dignity can handle walking back into the store carrying armadillo bedroom slippers, that is). I'm assuming these people were free to have done the same thing with Oprah's gift.

To me, complaining about a gift of a brand-new car is a little like winning the Publisher's Clearing House Sweepstakes, then handing the van driver a bill for running over your azaleas. You might have every right to do so (after all, they were *your* azaleas), but the driver also just brought you a check for a million dollars. With that kind of money, you could buy your own nursery!

Maybe it's just me, but in our day it seemed people were far more appreciative of what they had been given. Maybe that was because we, or our parents and grandparents, had gone through times of war, famine, recessions and, for some, a major depression.

Today some people think they're "doing without" if they can't afford to buy dessert. Back then "thank you" didn't sound like a foreign language. People instinctively said it whenever someone did something nice for them. In fact, people even routinely sent thank-you cards to acknowledge someone's generosity. They didn't ignore gifts or the kindnesses shown to them. There wasn't such a sense of entitlement. They were more grateful and they showed it more often and more sincerely. They also had good memories of the generosity of others. There was far less of that "what has anyone done for me lately?" attitude.

But don't misunderstand. I'm not at all implying that any of the people who were given those new cars on Oprah's show had a sense of entitlement. I'm sure they are all good, hardworking folks who just needed a little help. I am also sure that down deep they were all thankful for the gift, even in spite of any problems or misunderstandings.

The point I'm making is simply this—there does seem to be a growing number of people today who are going through their lives joyless and unsatisfied, complaining about what they don't have without taking an honest inventory of everything they do have. Martin Luther once said, "Unthankfulness is theft." I think he might have been right. When we complain about what we lack without acknowledging all we have right in front of us, it is a little like stealing. And the sad part is, when we live our lives this way, the one we're ultimately robbing is ourselves.

> **If the only prayer you ever say in your entire life**
> **is thank you, it will be enough.**
> —Meister Eckhart

Retirement Community

How beautiful it is to do nothing,
and then rest afterward.
—Spanish Proverb

I have to say that the thought of moving to a retirement community has never really interested me. I haven't reached retirement age yet, but for years I've been convinced that to feel youthful and vital, one needs to be surrounded by young people.

But I think I might need to back up and rethink that for a moment.

After having lived next door to teenagers who seemed to have no direction in their lives, throwing parties while their parents are away, playing loud music till all hours of the night, walking down the street with their boom boxes blaring, and constantly revving their car engines, a retirement community doesn't seem so bad anymore.

Also in a retirement community you usually don't have people "trying to find themselves." Most of the residents are pretty comfortable with who they are. By the time you reach retirement age, you don't have to prove anything to anyone. You're comfortable in your skin. It might not be as tight a fit as it once was, but you're comfortable.

Retirement communities don't have to deal with gangs either. You won't see "AARP" spray-painted on the side of buildings, and no one will be standing on the corner peddling B_{12} shots.

Another advantage to living in a retirement community is that older citizens usually do realize the importance of showing good manners and consideration for one's neighbors. Their wild parties are over by nine o'clock, and the only mess they make is when someone pours too much Epsom salt in the Jacuzzi.

I have to admit the advertisements for some of these retirement communities today are pretty enticing. They picture golf courses, waterfalls, gardens, community centers with monthly guest speakers covering a variety of interesting topics, holiday parties, and much more. Some of these places offer restaurant facilities and shopping, as well as a post office, drug store, and other business offices. They are their own village. Some even offer gyms and personal trainers.

And the people pictured on the brochures don't even look old anymore. They look youthful and vibrant, and they seem to be having the time of their lives enjoying all the activities and spending their children's inheritance.

So on second thought, when my husband and I get ready

to retire, maybe we'll look into moving to a retirement community. We like peace and quiet. We like mannerly neighbors. And we're usually in bed by nine o'clock, anyway. As for the Epsom-salt Jacuzzi? I guess it's like they say: You don't know if you'll like it unless you try.

The best time to start thinking about your retirement is before the boss does.
—Source unknown

Road Signs for the Middle-Ager and Beyond

No Outlet (shopping)

Watch Out for Falling Parts

Reduced Estrogen Ahead

No Dumping (We've all got enough problems of our own.)

No Passing Zone (Looks like you'll have to keep your kidney stone a little longer.)

Bridge May Freeze (Dentures, too, so use caution when eating ice cream.)

Watch Downhill Speed (You may be over the hill, but you haven't come to the Stop sign yet. So slow down and enjoy the rest of the journey.)

39

Welcome Mat

**_We cannot always oblige; but we can always
speak obligingly._**
—Voltaire

I live in Tennessee now. I grew up, married, and raised our
family in California, but we moved to Tennessee a few years
ago. They're polite here in Tennessee. In fact, the national
news recently covered a robbery that took place here in the
Volunteer State, where the alleged perpetrator, an elderly
man, apologized to the clerk before robbing the store. Talk
about Southern hospitality. It isn't something you just read
about in books. It's real. People out here really do take their
manners seriously.

When we first moved to the South, we were amazed at all
the kindnesses that were so generously shown to us by the
various people we encountered. Once, when my husband and
I were needing a large dogwood tree (an anniversary/house-
warming gift from good friend Diantha Ain) delivered to our
house, a man at the nursery pulled up next to us in his
pickup truck and asked if we were the ones who needed help

transporting a tree to our home. When we told him we were, he loaded it into his truck and then followed us to our house. The entire time that he was loading it up and driving behind us en route to our home, we just assumed that he worked for the nursery. But come to find out, he was just another customer! We tried to tip him for his kindness and time, but he refused. He did it, he said, just to "help out."

Another time, when my daughter-in-law, Crystal, and I had bought a television set and were trying to load the giant box into our car, a lady driving down the parking aisle noticed us struggling, then pulled up and asked if we wanted to put the box in the back of her truck so she could take it to our house for us. Just at that moment, though, we had finally managed to get the box to fit into the car, so we turned down her offer. In Los Angeles, if someone had offered to drive a newly purchased television set to our house, we probably would have just heard the sound of burning rubber as they peeled out of the parking lot with the box, heading in the opposite direction of our home. But the woman who offered to help us was just showing us her natural Southern hospitality.

I like living in a place where friendly, considerate people abound, where the notion of folks helping other folks isn't just a fantasy, where strangers are made to feel comfortable and welcome in an unfamiliar setting. Sure, there are plenty of people who use and abuse the kindness of others, who take advantage of someone's generosity and kindness, who may even exaggerate or fabricate their need or desperation and prey on the goodwill of society. But that still shouldn't stop us from showing good ol' Southern hospitality to others no matter what part of the country, or world, we happen to live in. It's wise to ask questions, and certainly, if we've been burned before, it might make us more selective of where and to whom we offer our help, but it shouldn't make us stop meeting the real needs of those who happen to cross our path throughout our day.

My mother was always hospitable. She never cared if more people than she had planned on showed up for dinner. She would simply "throw some more beans in the pot." And she always put herself last, believing that guests should have the best of whatever you had to offer. For every one person who might have taken unfair advantage of that quality, there were a host of other appreciative ones who will be eternally grateful for her kindness.

So yes, I must say that all of this Southern hospitality has been nice. The older we get, the more kindness and respect seem to matter. But the South doesn't hold the patent on those qualities. I've met nice people in the North, in the East, and in the West. There are plenty of nice people in big cities like Los Angeles, Chicago, and New York, too. It just seems to be a little more of an epidemic in the South. And that's one epidemic I don't think any of us would want to stop.

Clothes and manners do not make the man;
but, when he is made,
they greatly improve his appearance.
—Henry Ward Beecher

40

Not Looking Back

Save the Earth, it's the only planet
with chocolate.
—Bumper sticker

Have you fallen into the trap of saying to yourself that as soon as this or that happens, then you'll be happy? If only my daughter would get her life straightened out. If only my son called a little more often. If only my neighbor wasn't such a grump. If only I didn't have so many bills. If only I had a better car. If only I could afford to take that trip I've always dreamed about. If only my husband didn't leave. If only my wife was less critical. If only my friends were more caring. If only, if only, if only.

Do you know that while you're busy waiting for life to be "perfect," your imperfect life keeps marching on day after day, week after week, year after year? Time doesn't stop for life to straighten itself out. We just have to accept the fact that life is very rarely a perfect proposition. So don't waste another minute waiting for it to be. Those "perfect" circumstances might not ever come along, and while you're wasting your time waiting for them, all you're going to get is older and less happy.

And don't waste another minute pining about yesterday and what might have been. It very well might have been, but it wasn't. No matter how much we beg for yesterday to return, it's irretrievable. Life offers no rewrites. Even a minute ago is too far gone to ever bring back. Whatever happened, good or bad, fun or boring, worthwhile or wasted, is now history. The only thing we have the power over is today. Even tomorrow is unpredictable.

That's the nice thing, though, about middle age. By the time we've made it this far, we've (hopefully) learned a lot from the past—to influence the decisions we make today and to improve our lives tomorrow. We've learned not to let other people's opinions affect us as much as they did in our youth. By this stage in our lives we've had to maneuver our way through some of life's more rocky places. We've won a few and lost some, too. We've been praised, blamed, uplifted, demeaned, coddled, kicked around, loved, and rejected. If we were paying attention through it all, we've learned a thing or two about ourselves, others, and life.

One of the most important things we've learned is that all those losses and hurts, the ones that were so painful it felt like we might not ever survive them, somehow didn't destroy us. We survived not one, not two, not twenty, but every single one of them. We wouldn't still be here if we hadn't. Like Reinhold Niebuhr said in his oft-quoted prayer, we accepted those things that we could not change, changed those things that we could, and had the wisdom (most of the time) to know the difference. Maybe life didn't turn out exactly the way we wanted it, and maybe some of our survival may have required setting boundaries that were necessary for our own health and peace of mind. But through God's mercy, we made it to this point of our life. That is no small accomplishment. It's called endurance, and if we're still around today, we were apparently blessed with a good deal of it.

Our parents and grandparents knew how to endure. When the going got rough, they hung tough. They didn't pull over to the side of life's road and whine about how tricky the lane changes were or how many times they got cut off by another driver. They knew the road of life was treacherous for all of us at some point. They didn't expect it to be otherwise. They just taught themselves how to adapt and take things as they come. Many of them lived through the Great Depression. They survived two world wars. They lived through political scandals, weather disasters, and black-and-white TV. They knew how to adjust their sails. They knew how to persevere, hang on to hope, and never ever give in to doubt or fear. They were true survivors.

So don't give away any more of today's energy and promise fretting over the pain or disappointment of the past. Deal with it if you haven't already, face the truth of your hurts and failures, confront who you must, forgive who you need to, set healthy boundaries with those who have a history of hurting you, and then move on. Be a survivor, too.

Finish each day and be done with it. You have done what you could; some blunders and absurdities have crept in; forget them as soon as you can. Tomorrow is a new day; you shall begin it serenely and with too high a spirit to be encumbered with your old nonsense.
—Ralph Waldo Emerson

41

Vote for Who?

Being president is a lot like running a cemetery.
You've got a lot of people under you and
nobody's listening.
—Bill Clinton

I don't think I'll run for president. Nobody has asked me yet, but even if I were to be approached by the nominating committee of either political party, I don't think I'd accept the invitation. The pay is fine. Actually, it's more than fine. But there are too many requirements for running the most powerful nation in the world. For one thing, I'm pretty sure you can't sleep in. If you're still in bed past noon, someone is bound to be looking for you. And if you try to catch a quick catnap between your thoughts during a State of the Union address, the picture is sure to hit the front page of every newspaper in the country.

I've also come to realize that it's virtually impossible to please everyone, no matter how hard you work at it. If you sign this bill, the Republicans get mad. If you sign that bill, the Democrats get upset. If you don't do anything, the independents will be picketing in front of the White House. You can do your best to make everyone happy, and you're still going to make someone unhappy. Sometimes you might even make half the country unhappy. Like Lyndon Johnson once said, "If one morning I walked on top of the water across the Potomac River, the headline that afternoon would read, 'President Can't Swim.'"

I am, however, fascinated with how the political machine works. It's fun to look for spin in the press or try to see the bigger picture in difficult decisions made by either party. I also find it quite interesting to see how hard all the political parties work to win the senior and baby boomer vote. Beyond playing oldies tunes at some of their rallies, the candidates will address topics like whether or not Social Security will be there for us when we retire (even though many of us have been paying into it for decades), and they'll make pledges to make our streets safer, cut our taxes, keep interest rates at a reasonable level, give us better prescription drug coverage, fund more medical research, build better roads, and control the rate of inflation. The list goes on and on.

It's hard to keep track of all the promises the candidates routinely make to us when they're running for office. So why do they go to so much trouble to get our votes? Because we are a force to be reckoned with. Not only are we great in number, but we vote. We actually show up at the polls and go through the process. We don't let much of anything keep us away from the polls. We send donations to our respective political parties. We tune in to the debates. We call up the talk shows. We read (sometimes word for word) the political literature that is mailed to us. Most of us are very much involved in the political process.

MTV can hype the youth vote, run super-slick ads trying to get millions of young adults to register, but on election night, we're still the ones showing up. In rain, snow, or rush-hour traffic. Or we mail in our ballots ahead of time. When it comes to our right to vote, we take it very seriously. Maybe that's because we have a very good understanding of what went into winning that right, and we don't take the sacrifice of those who went before us lightly.

But I still don't think I'd ever want to be president. It's just too hard to run a country and still keep up with all my soaps.

There are advantages to being president. The day after I was elected, I had my high school grades classified.
—Ronald Reagan

42

On Purpose

Life is a promise; fulfill it.
—Mother Teresa

How many times in our lives have we apologized or had someone apologize to us for things that weren't done "on purpose"?

"I didn't hurt your feelings on purpose," someone will say to us. *"But I had to tell you the truth about your hair. Was it really your intention for it to come out that particular shade of orange?"*

Or they'll run over our toes with their grocery cart and then apologize. *"I'm sorry. I didn't do that on purpose. Let me just back up over them again and then I'll be out of your way."*

Whether the apology is sincere or not, we may never really know for sure. Without getting inside someone's head, it's hard to know what they do on purpose and what they truly do accidentally. Some of us don't even see when our own actions are very much on purpose.

There is something, though, that we should all do "on purpose," and that's live our lives. None of us should want to just wander about from decade to decade, career to career, relationship to relationship. We should want, even demand, more out of our lives. We are here for a reason, and we should find that reason.

What is it that you feel driven to accomplish in your life? It doesn't matter how old you are. It's never too late to fulfill your purpose.

Ask yourself this: If you were to make a "To-Do" list for your life, what would be on it? Where would you like to go? Whom would you like to meet? What would you like to learn? What have you always wanted to do? What field have you always wanted to work in? What charity have you always had a heart for?

Think about it, then jot down some of your goals, aspirations, and things that you still hope to accomplish in your lifetime. This is your "To-Do List for Life":

1.
2.
3.
4.
5.
6.
7.
8.
9.
10.

Now that you know at least ten of your lifelong desires, start doing them one at a time, or at least attempting them, and as you accomplish each one, check it off. What you do with your life is up to you. It will be as fulfilling or as unful-filling as you allow it to be. If you've got today, you've got the time to make a difference.

Dost thou love life? Then do not squander time, for that is the stuff life is made of.
—Benjamin Franklin

43

How to Have a Happy Birthday

- ✿ Give yourself a present.
- ✿ Call an old friend that you haven't talked to in a long time.
- ✿ Take a few of your favorite old photos out of their albums or shoe boxes and prominently display them somewhere in your home.
- ✿ Have someone else take your picture. If no one is around, go to a studio (Wal-Mart, Sears, and many other discount department stores have reasonably priced photo studios) and get your picture taken. Even those photo booths at malls would cost you only a few dollars for four poses. Or if you have a camera, stroll to a nearby park and ask someone to take your picture. Most people will gladly accommodate your request. It doesn't matter how you get your picture taken, but document this special day with a photo.

✿ Make this day a day of favorites. Wear your favorite shirt, watch your favorite television shows, eat your favorite foods, talk to your favorite people, read your favorite book. It's your day—treat yourself to the things you enjoy.

✿ Tell others what you'd like for your birthday. If you don't get it, don't be disappointed. Just look at it as an opportunity to treat your own body and mind with a little "thank-you gift" for all they've done for you, then go out and buy it yourself.

✿ If whoever you're hoping will call you today doesn't call by 6 P.M., call him or her. Once the two of you start talking, you'll forget all about which one of you had to do the dialing.

✿ Look in the mirror and tell yourself that you are one fine-looking person for whatever age you happen to be.

✿ Buy a birthday card or gift for someone else whose birthday is close to yours. Giving to others has a residual effect of making you feel good, too.

✿ Pick some flowers, put them in a vase, and display them where you can see them all day long.

✿ Look through catalogs and circle everything you'd like to have. You may never buy any of it, but it's fun to dream.

✿ Share at least one good memory with someone, even if it's your pharmacist.

✿ Write in your journal what you learned about yourself and life throughout the previous year.

✿ Sing "Happy Birthday" to yourself at least one time all the way through, and smile while you're doing this.

❀ Hide a dollar in your house for you to find next year on your birthday. It'll be good exercise for your brain to spend the next 365 days trying to remember where you hid it. If you do this every year for the rest of your life, and always forget where you've hidden the money, think of all the fun your heirs will have discovering all those dollar bills.

❀ Never forget that on this day someone very special was born. You.

44

Without You

"One man's life touches so many others,
when he's not there it leaves an
awfully big hole."
—Clarence from *It's a Wonderful Life*

Have you ever been in one of those melancholy moods where you found yourself feeling insignificant? Maybe you've even wondered what life might have been like had you never been born. You've asked yourself if there would be, as Clarence said in *It's a Wonderful Life*, an awfully big hole where you were meant to be.

The answer is yes, there would be an awfully big hole. We don't always realize that, though. Too often we think if we didn't make some amazing medical discovery, or were instrumental in achieving world peace, or some other incredible feat, then we had no worth. But the proof of our importance to this world is most often found in small ways.

In the movie *Saving Private Ryan*, Private Ryan spent his life trying to prove to himself that he was worthy of the ultimate sacrifice that was paid by the soldiers who lost their lives trying to save his. He carried tremendous guilt and never quite felt worthy of the trade. But by the end of the movie, his wife assures him that the sacrifice of those men wasn't in vain, because Private Ryan was a good man. He was important in the lives of his family.

No, we may not change the world by discovering the cure for cancer, but those cards, phone calls, and visits that we gave to a friend who was diagnosed with cancer may have been the hope he or she needed to hang on, to keep fighting and ultimately win the battle. Maybe we never held a political office that enabled us to create policies that would help save the world, but those toys we gave away to a needy child that one Christmas may have meant the whole world to that boy or girl.

We don't always see the importance of the small acts of kindnesses that we do. We brush off these little niceties, almost embarrassed at their apparent insignificance, telling ourselves that anybody could have done what we did. But the simple truth is, nobody else was doing it, at least not at that time. We saw the need of one single person in one single moment and we acted.

If a survey was ever taken of people whose lives had been miraculously changed, we might be surprised at how many of them would say that the turning point came as a result of one small act of kindness, either given by someone they knew or a total stranger.

Do you remember how the "buddy system" worked when you were younger? If a group of you were going swimming, hiking, mountain biking, or doing some other outdoor sport, the leader always made sure that everyone had a buddy with them at all times. You were assigned someone to watch out for you in case anything went wrong, and you watched out for them. That's because no one person could keep their eye on the entire group at every moment.

The same is true in life. None of us can be there for everyone. It's a physical, financial, and emotional impossibility. But I'm sure those we have helped, either financially or emotionally, those we gave a kind word to, or a monetary gift, or showed any kindness in any way, are forever grateful that we happened to come along at the precise moment of their need. And we'll be forever grateful for those who happened along in our times of need.

So, yes, there would be an awfully big hole. From the very first day of your life, you've been affecting people. Your parents, your extended family, your friends, even people you didn't know that well, or at all for that matter. Your birth may have meant everything to your parents. That first home run you hit in Little League may have been the proudest moment in your father's life. When you were in the eighth grade you may have thought you were just warming a chair, but that smile you gave to the boy sitting behind you in class may have been the only one he got all semester. The time you defended a friend who was being picked on in school was no small thing. It took courage to stand up for someone whom everyone else was making fun of. Think it went unnoticed? That girl is forty-eight now, and to this day she can still recite your words verbatim. You've been making an impact on people your entire life, you just don't know it.

We may not know until we get to heaven just how many lives we've positively affected simply by our being here. And since we're all still around, that can only mean there are plenty more lives waiting to be affected by our presence, too.

An insignificant life? Hardly.

> **"You see, George, you really have had a wonderful life."**
> —Clarence from *It's a Wonderful Life*

Go On and Laugh!

There's More Than One Way to Get a Hot Meal!

Who says growing old isn't fun? Sure, each day brings its own disturbing surprises, but aging has its benefits, too. Martha Bolton believes that the older you get, the smarter you become, and she's only slightly kidding when she offers her hilarious idea of scratch-and-taste samples in the cooking magazines.

*Cooking With Hot Flashes:
And Other Ways to Make Middle Age Profitable*

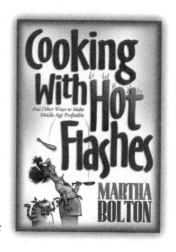

Living, Laughing, and Loving After Forty!

A full-time comedy writer for Bob Hope, Ann Jillian, and others, Martha Bolton's attitude is that when you can't stop the crow's-feet from walking all over your face, it's time to laugh about it. And that's her goal in this humorous yet insightful book on life after forty.

Didn't My Skin Used to Fit?

Give Your Mind a Break, Not a Breakdown

Instead of letting your thoughts give you a headache, use Martha's remedy—laugh! Finding the humor in life is what keeps us sane...and keeps the headaches at bay. This is a book that takes the premise that "laughter is the best medicine" very seriously.

I Think, Therefore I Have a Headache!

◆ BETHANYHOUSE